Physi  ion

Models for Aligning Financial Goals and Incentives

Second Edition

Kenneth M. Hekman, FACMPE

Medical Group Management Association
104 Inverness Terrace East
Englewood, CO 80112
(877) 275-6462
Web site: http://www.mgma.com

KENDALL/HUNT PUBLISHING COMPANY
4050 Westmark Drive   Dubuque, Iowa 52002

Medical Group
Management
Association

Medical Group Management Association (MGMA) publications are intended to provide current and accurate information and are designed to assist readers in becoming more familiar with the subject matter covered. Such publications are distributed with the understanding that MGMA does not render any legal, accounting or other professional advice that may be construed as specifically applicable to individual situations. No representations or warranties are made concerning the application of legal or other principles discussed by the authors to any specific factual situation, nor is any prediction made concerning how any particular judge, government official or other person will interpret or apply such principles. Specific factual situations should be discussed with professional advisors.

Cover photo courtesy of PhotoDisc, Inc

Item # 5912

Copyright © 2002 by the Medical Group Management Association

ISBN 1-56829-179-5

Printed in the United States of America
10   9   8   7   6   5   4   3   2

Contents

Chapter Overviews

1. Take the Money and Grumble   Robert Lowes

Physician compensation has a colorful history, beginning with traditions of payment in farm produce, to reluctant participation in insurance plans, and laced with a fairly consistent measure of discontent throughout. The opening chapter puts the subject in context, and sets the stage for an exploration of the facts as well as the feelings surrounding this timeless topic.

2. Compensation Principles   Kenneth M. Hekman

The foundational principles of physician compensation are outlined to give the reader an understanding of the relationship between work and pay for professionals.

- Money is a by-product of service
- Aligning incentives with the market and with strategic directions of the practice
- Information systems and the role of regular feedback
- The delicate balance of competing interests
- The role of benefits in the compensation picture
- Correlating compensation to work and conducting reality checks
- The wisdom of experience
  - It all has to come from somewhere
  - Collegiality grows
  - The value of simplicity
  - Don't confuse compensation formulas with management

3. Legal Aspects of Physician Compensation   Kenneth G. Hofman, J.D.

Since a significant portion of physician reimbursement comes from governmental programs, physicians and medical managers must be aware of a wide variety of legal constraints impacting physician compensation.

- Introduction to the Law
  - Fraud and Abuse
  - Stark laws
  - Inurement
- Applications
  - Group practice compensation
  - Hospital employment of physicians
  - Special hospital contracting issues

Traditional compensation models have responded to the fee-for-service reimbursement environment in which physicians are paid on the basis of their volume and intensity of care. This chapter outlines the components impacting how physicians get paid in the fee-for-service environment, how they can respond to the incentives of those components, and how groups can blend the motivations of a diverse group of physicians to accomplish corporate goals.

- Components
  - Fees
  - Payer mix
  - Coding
  - Competition
  - Intensity
  - Time Efficiency
  - Collection ratios
  - Overhead costs
  - Compensation systems
- The problems of prediction when all the targets are moving
- The myth of EWYK
- Case Examples
- Compensation Models

Working under capitation agreements requires physicians to respond to different incentives than they respond to under fee-for-service agreements. In this chapter we will explore the significant differences in incentives, with special attention to how those differences impact compensation policies and procedures. The data requirements, internal relationships within the group, and external referral relationships will be explored for their role in developing sound compensation systems.

- The Case for Action
- Mission Vision and Values
- Design Principles
- Compensation Plan Architecture
  - Base Plus Incentive
  - XYZ Plans
  - Performance Measures for Incentives
    - Clinical Productivity
    - Resource Utilization
    - Patient Satisfaction

- Quality
- Leadership and Citizenship
- Financial Structure for Incentives
- Incentive Plan Development
- Case Examples

6. A Checklist for Devising New Compensation Plans   Kenneth M. Hekman

The process of changing a compensation plan can be as important to its success at the design of the plan. In this chapter, we will examine the steps involved, as well as a few qualitative questions to ask along the way, to minimize the stress inherent in every change.

- Discerning when a formula change is necessary
- Who should be at the table
- Five steps
  1. Articulate what you want the compensation system to accomplish
  2. Look backward to compare how well the old system worked to accomplish the new goals
  3. Brainstorm how to better measure behaviors that support new goals
  4. Refine the model until you have agreement
  5. Evaluate its effectiveness in the real world

7. Design Variances   Kenneth M. Hekman

While most compensation systems have common foundations, the way they are applied may vary widely. In this chapter, we will examine some of the most prominent settings, and the considerations that might impact the design and implementation of compensation systems.

- Single-specialty groups
- Multi-specialty groups
- Hospital-owned practices
- Academic settings
- Rural communities
- Physician-extenders
- Part time physicians
- Officer compensation
- Opting out of call responsibilities

8. The ABCs of Gainsharing   Paul Davis and Majel Maes

Support staff can play a significant role in boosting revenues and containing costs in any medical practice setting. Aligning staff incentives with physician incentives can be a powerful force in maximizing compensation and achieving corporate goals. The Scanlon

Plan and its derivatives offer a fundamental model for comprehensive management. This chapter offers a glimpse of the theories and practices of gainsharing.

- What is gainsharing?
- Assumptions
- Business literacy
- Commitment

9. Implementation   Seth Garber, M.D.

A good model is only as good as its implementation. This chapter explores fourteen barriers to successful implementation of a new compensation system, and addresses how to prevent them from compromising the benefits of a proposed change.

10. Strategies for Improving Physician Compensation   Kenneth M. Hekman

The bottom line on physician compensation is how to improve the bottom line. In this chapter, we summarize group strategies and individual strategies for boosting compensation that are applicable to all medical practice environments. We also explore the trends that will shape compensation formulas in the future, and conclude with some timeless perspectives about the relationship between physician compensation and society.

- Individual strategies for working hard and working smart
- Group strategies for working hard and working smart
- Trends and perspectives

Appendix

Appendix 1 Development and Implementation of a New Physician Compensation Plan
Jane Parrish

Appendix 2 Transitioning Employed Physicians from Fixed Salaries to Production-Based Compensation in a Large, Hospital-Affiliated Multi-Specialty Group Practice
James R. Wurts, FACMPE

Appendix 3 A New Paradigm in Academic Health Centers: Productivity-Based Physician Compensation
Margie C. Andreae, MD, and Gary L. Freed, MD, MPH

About the Author

Kenneth M. Hekman is the president of Hekman & Associates, Inc., a healthcare consulting firm based in Holland, Michigan. Mr. Hekman is the author of *Buying, Selling and Merging a Medical Practice,* and a co-author of *Physician Driven Health Plans.* He has served as a business strategist and as a mentor to physicians and administrators in medical practices nationwide for over two decades. He holds a Masters degree in Business Administration and is a Fellow in the American College of Medical Practice Executives. Mr. Hekman also serves as an advisor to healthcare organizations in Eastern Europe and Central America. Additional information can be found at *www.Hekmangroup.com.*

About the Contributors

Paul Davis serves as president of the nonprofit Scanlon Leadership Network. Majel C. Maes is the Network's director of Programs and Administration. The Network provides networking opportunities for member organizations located throughout North America and serves as a worldwide clearinghouse of Scanlon related research, thought and practice. Scanlon Leadership Network has been called the "best kept secret in American business," and "The best idea of the 20th Century" (*Training Magazine*). They can be reached at Scanlon Leadership Network, 2875 Northwind Drive, Suite 121, East Lansing, MI 48823 (517) 332-8927, Email: office@scanlonleader.org, website *www.scanlonleader.org.*

Seth Garber, M.D. is a physician consultant with the Health Care and Group Benefits Practice of Mercer Human Resource Consulting, and is the Clinical Quality Representative for Kaiser Permanente in Portland, Oregon. His consulting focuses on governance and compensation issues for medical groups, and on analyzing and improving the effectiveness of medical management for employers. Seth is a board-certified internist. He received his B.A., Summa Cum Laude, from Harvard College and his M.D. from Harvard Medical School. He also completed the Advanced Management Program of the Harvard Business School.

Kenneth G. Hofman is a member in Miller, Johnson, Snell & Cummiskey, P.L.C. in Grand Rapids, Michigan, a full-service law firm with a very active health law practice. He has over 16 years of experience representing physicians. His clients range from large, multi-specialty groups to small, single specialty groups. He also enjoys his involvement with non-profit organizations, one of which maintains a primary care clinic dedicated to the health care needs of the central city of Grand Rapids.

Robert Lowes is the midwest editor for *Medical Economics.* He is based in St. Louis, Missouri, and his contribution is reprinted with permission from *Medical Economics' 75th Anniversary Issue,* October 19, 1998, © 1998 by *Medical Economics.*

Deborah L. Walker is a principal with BOEHM/WALKER Associates, a healthcare consulting firm based in Southern California that specializes in medical practice management and physician incentive compensation. She is known for her ability to achieve sustainable organizational changes and productivity improvements to enable a competitive position in the managed care market. Ms. Walker earned her MBA degree from UCLA, she is a Fellow of the American College of Medical Practice Executives, and she is a Ph.D. candidate at The Peter F. Drucker Graduate School of Management, Claremont Graduate University. Ms. Walker is an accomplished executive with more than 22 years experience in healthcare. She has authored numerous articles on medical practice management issues and she is a frequent speaker at national healthcare forums.

Preface

Few issues capture physicians' attention in group practices more firmly than their compensation. It is symbolic of power and self-worth, of status and position. Although shades of altruism may have drawn physicians into the profession, their sizable education debts, high self-expectations, and collegiality with peers draw them to the bottom line soon enough. Physicians have typically enjoyed incomes near the top of the economic structure in the United States, but the issue is seldom whether they earn enough. In group settings in particular, the issue is more poignantly seen as whether each one earns enough *relative to colleagues*. Fairness is more critical, in most doctors' minds, than magnitude. Compensation systems symbolize equity in a medical group. They govern how the medical revenues will be split, and therefore have an impact directly or indirectly on just about every decision the group must make.

It should come as no surprise, therefore, that compensation systems are placed under the microscope with regularity, and that there is no such thing as a perfect system. They are mathematical models for something that is not mathematical in nature. Compensation systems are at the heart of trust among colleagues in a medical group—trust that spills over from economics to clinical issues, from financial decisions to personal and professional relationships. Compensation is where the rubber hits the road—where group decisions have an intensely personal impact.

Few professions have seen such a sea of change in financial management as have physicians. The complexity of medical reimbursement has been shaped and reshaped by dramatic forces in public policy, international markets, science and technology. Physicians were rewarded for centuries on the basis of their medical interventions, and offered little incentive to contain health care costs through prevention. With the advent of managed care and all its derivatives, however, physicians are now being rewarded for the things they were formerly not rewarded for, and *vice versa*. Physician compensation discussions have become confused and disjointed affairs, leaving doctors and their managers bewildered and uncertain as to whether the pie is being split fairly or not.

This book cannot—indeed, no book can—solve all these problems. Our goals are much more modest ones, and perhaps more achievable ones: to share insights about group dynamics, examine the theory and practice of wealth distribution, look at a few models and examples, and challenge readers to wrestle with both the symbolism and the methods of physician compensation. This book is designed to inform your experimentation, rather than to deliver a perfect model. Its purposes are to sensitize you to what is at stake in physician compensation, and to look for intended and unintended consequences of a wide range of medical management decisions.

Since compensation is such a multifaceted issue, it was only natural to assemble perspectives from multiple points of view. We have gathered insights from consultants actively engaged in developing sound compensation strategies. You will learn of the history, beginning with payment in the form of farm produce; of the legal constraints, of several different models in alternative markets, of employee gain-sharing concepts, and of implementation issues from a doctor's point of view. The final chapter offers specific strategies for compensation improvement that can be applied at both the group level and the individual physician level.

You will notice the different points of view of the contributing authors, both in their content and their form. But this is far from a collection of independent ideas. The chapters are linked—indeed, the authors are linked—by a common respect for the profession, for the role compensation systems play in groups, and for the impact sound principles can play in delivering both high quality care and responsible economic value. The compensation models must change as markets change, but I hope you gain an enduring respect for the tenuous and critical dynamics at work in designing physician compensation systems, and of their impact on physicians, their support staff, their patients and our society.

Justice and fairness are worthy goals in designing physician compensation systems, but so are compassion, competitiveness and compromise. I encourage you to glean the insights from seasoned consultants shared in this book, *and to keep a healthy perspective.* The first word and the last word on physician compensation is simply this: Some things—a lot of things—are more important than money.

Ken Hekman

1

Take the Money and Grumble

ROBERT LOWES

In the early 1940s, Michigan doctors faced a choice. They could embrace one of the nation's first Blue Shield plans and accept its checks for treating autoworkers who'd signed up for the newfangled prepaid medical care. Or doctors could cling to the status quo—relying on patients to pay the bills themselves.

A sizable minority chose tradition, hanging plaques in their waiting rooms stating defiantly that no checks from the likes of Blue Shield would be accepted. A third-party payer violated the patient-physician relationship, they maintained. But droves of autoworkers with Blue Shield coverage made that position untenable.

So the traditionalists made a concession: They continued to shun the checks, but they accepted insurance company cash, hand-delivered to their offices by Blue Shield employees.

That's among the events documented in a history of Blue Cross and Blue Shield by Robert M. Cunningham Jr. and his son, Robert Cunningham III. Doctors felt that health insurance was an intrusion on their practice. "But," as one Blues official told the Cunninghams, "it was not an intrusion to take the money."

And take the money they have. By now, third-party payers account for roughly 85 percent of private practitioners' income.

It's good money, too. By making medical care affordable for America's working class, employer-paid health insurance has generated fees doctors wouldn't have otherwise collected. And through Medicare, doctors get paid for treating many elderly people who previously had either lacked adequate care or received it gratis.

At the same time, doctors complain louder than ever about the intrusions of third-party payers. Preauthorization for surgery, gatekeepers, formularies, fee schedules, peer review panels—the behavior modification practiced by third-party payers has driven some doctors to retire early, some to group up for defensive purposes, others to unionize, and still others to form their own HMOs to regain the upper hand.

Many issues that pushed hot buttons in 1923, when this magazine began covering the office-practice scene, continue to push them in 1998. The piano player in "Casablanca" had it right: The fundamentals still apply.

YOU CAN REPOSSESS A SOFA, BUT NOT A NEWBORN

A cartoon in a 1939 issue of *Medical Economics* shows a farm boy giving a doctor a gallon of blackberries in partial payment of his family's bill. The doctor forces out a thank you. On a nearby table sit 10 gallons of blackberries from other patients.

It's easy to romanticize the self-pay era of medicine, but a glut of blackberries was only one of the hassles. Collecting from patients was a heavy burden, says Robert Cunningham III.

"For one thing, a doctor had to evaluate each patient's ability to pay," he says. "Should he charge his standard fee, discount it, offer an installment plan, or simply write off the bill as charity?"

The poor stood a good chance of receiving free care. Many doctors, such as retired general surgeon Charles C. Huntley of Missoula, Montana, exulted in generosity. Huntley, who began practicing medicine in Avoca, Iowa, in 1931, had a Christmas tradition of selecting the most deserving patient with the largest past-due bill and mailing it to him marked "Paid in full."

"I hope it gave the recipient as much pleasure as I derived from the giving," says Huntley.

Huntley and others also accepted barter from patients hard up for cash. "In my first year of practice, half of my income was farm produce," says Huntley. "Eggs, chicken, beef, butter—we didn't starve."

Deadbeats were the scourge of medicine. "People who never paid their bills would go through the phone book and look for listings of new doctors," says practice management consultant Lee Scroggins in Cincinnati. "Once their past-due amount got too high, they moved on to the next sucker." Local medical societies circulated deadbeat lists to provide advance warning.

Many a no-pay evolves from a slow-pay, and by the Roaring Twenties, America had institutionalized slow-pay in the form of the installment plan. That was good for furniture sales, but not for house calls. You could repossess a sofa, but as one wag observed, you couldn't repossess a baby you'd delivered. Furthermore, patients who frantically called a doctor about a loved one's high fever didn't treat the doctor's bill like an emergency five months later.

House Calls for Cash, and Other Ploys

In a country enamored with credit, physicians have had to take a more businesslike approach toward collections. But in the '20s, there remained the old-fashioned country doctor who seemed bored (or perhaps repelled) by the subject. Charles Huntley recalls that he riled patients because he was the first doctor in his Iowa community to send out bills. Apparently, his colleagues hadn't read the provocative 1924 article: "Does it pay to collect?"

The forward-thinking physician of that time mailed out not only a past-due bill but also a collection letter, a considerable investment of psychic energy to push patients into the paying column. When letters didn't work, one doctor made a house call to "treat" a case of slow-payitis.

A collection agency became the last resort, but this approach backfired on occasion. Some unscrupulous agencies bilked doctors, and others hounded patients with midnight phone calls that did nothing to polish the physician's image.

To avoid the headaches of collection, smart doctors got their money up front. One Aurora, Illinois, practitioner discounted his fees 33 percent if patients paid cash on the spot. A New England physician had a stack of blank checks handy for solvent patients. Another doctor simply kept a woven basket on his desk and encouraged factory workers to toss in a dollar bill each visit. He put four children through college that way.

Schemes to encourage prompt payment grew more sophisticated. Bank loans for surgical procedures gained popularity in the 1950s. A doctor would suggest that a cash-strapped patient take advantage of a local bank's special loan plan—and then hand him an application form.

The credit-card revolution created a variation on the bank loan. By accepting plastic, a doctor could receive his fee within days, minus a small percentage of what the card company collected. "Initially, many doctors thought it was cheesy," says Lee Scroggins, "but plastic took off in the 1980s when people used it for co-pays and surgery not covered by insurance." This year, 7 percent of consumers used some sort of plastic to pay their out-of-pocket expenses to physicians.

VOLUNTARY HEALTH INSURANCE: THE LESSER OF TWO EVILS

The challenge of collecting from patients was a symptom of a more deep-seated problem in American health care. In the self-pay system, too many people couldn't afford to go to the doctor or hospital, and rising health costs only made things worse. One landmark study in the '30s showed that only half of lower-income families received medical care.

Spreading the financial burden through health insurance was an obvious solution. The question was, would America adopt a national compulsory program—as had Germany and Great Britain—or would it go the voluntary, private-sector route?

The American Medical Association lobby helped bar the door to national health insurance, stigmatizing it for decades as the embodiment of Communism. But to AMA chroniclers, what the organization really feared was a shift from the solo doctor who charged whatever fees he liked to groups of salaried doctors paid through capitation.

Meanwhile, voluntary health insurance made inroads. Immigrants formed societies to pay doctors a fixed amount per year for health care, according to medical historian William Rothstein at the University of Maryland. A few doctors organized clubs of prepaid patients. Lumber and mining camps paid monthly fees to doctors to care for workers in "contract practices" (criticized by the AMA as too commercial).

Modern health insurance, though, was born in 1929, when an executive at Baylor University in Dallas conceived a plan to guarantee local school teachers three weeks of hospital care if they paid $6 apiece per year, in advance. Communities nationwide quickly adopted the Dallas hospitalization plan, later known as Blue Cross.

But what about the doctor's bill? California physicians, backed by their state association, solved that problem in 1939 by forming the first Blue Shield program. The plan called for subscribers, whose earnings had to be $3,000 or less per year, to pay $1.70 per month for complete coverage. Participating doctors were paid on a fee-for-service basis, and fees were calculated in units worth $1.75 each—the going rate for an office visit-minus a discount.

Physicians proceeded to launch Blue Shield plans nationwide, and enrollment skyrocketed from 700,000 in 1942 to 10.2 million in 1948. World War II fertilized this dramatic growth. The federal government froze wages, but companies were allowed to keep workers happy by offering benefits such as health coverage.

Many doctors, like the "no checks" plaque-hangers in Michigan, initially felt threatened by voluntary health insurance. They believed the AMA line from the early 1930s that it would pave the way toward group practice and socialized medicine. But Blue Shield eventually won even the AMA's support. A voluntary health insurance plan, the argument went, was the lesser of two evils—if it succeeded, it could make a national health plan unnecessary. People who couldn't afford health care would become paying patients, while doctors would enjoy a simpler life.

"Collection troubles will be passé," predicted California Blue Shield supporters in 1939. What's more, doctors called the shots at Blue Shield plans, as opposed to the commercial insurance companies moving into health care. But the lesser of two evils still confronted doctors with evils: more paperwork, more telephone calls, and higher payrolls, recalls retired practice management consultant Clayton L. Scroggins (Lee's father), who went into the business in 1945. "Going from direct payment to third-party payment could easily triple the number of employees you needed," says the elder Scroggins.

Insurers also began peering over the shoulders of doctors. Even Blue Shield plans, for all their physician friendliness, began to look like adversaries. James E. Bryan, a New Jersey Blue Shield administrator, lamented in 1955 that too many Blue plans conducted wasteful audits and loaded contracts with legalistic gobbledygook.

"Some Blue Shield directors are beginning to treat all doctors and subscribers like potential crooks—merely to trap the occasional sharpie," Bryan wrote in these pages. The "sharpies" were doctors who, as Robert Cunningham III notes, milked Blue Shield by raising fees for insured patients so they could collect the insurance payment and—through balance billing—a fat check from the patient. How much of a minority the sharpies constituted remains a matter of debate. "Doctors almost always accepted what the insurance company determined they should get," recalls Clayton Scroggins. On the other hand, 17,000 Blue Shield members in Colorado canceled their membership over alleged fee-gouging in a year's time during the mid-1940s.

MEDICARE: MORE MONEY, FEWER RASPBERRIES

When Medicare went into effect on July 1, 1966, elderly patients of an Illinois GP asked whether he would refuse to see them anymore since the AMA had vilified the legislation. "I had to reassure them that doctors aren't on strike and that I'm certainly not refusing to take anyone," he said.

It was another example of take the money and grumble. Organized medicine had branded Medicare as socialized medicine, but the program was lucrative all the same. "I'll urge first-class care on all my elderly patients without worrying about breaking them or myself financially," said a Michigan internist.

The Johnson administration placated physicians by giving them what many have called an open checkbook. Medicare fees would be based on physicians' customary and prevailing charges in a given locale (an open door for fee inflation). Furthermore, doctors could either bill the government—and receive Uncle Sam's check—or bill the patient, who would then seek Medicare reimbursement. If doctors billed the government—taking assignment, in insurance parlance—they had to content themselves with whatever Medicare defined as a reasonable charge. But if they billed the patient, they could charge more than Medicare allowed.

"There was always the chance the patient would spend his Medicare check on a new roof, but the seniors were good about paying," says Lee Scroggins. Today, Medicare's financial incentives virtually eliminate non-assignment.

Medicare was a big reason why doctors' incomes rose 43 percent between 1965 and 1970, compared to roughly 25 percent from 1960 to 1965. Hefty increases in Medicare fees alarmed government officials, who soon wondered if the program would go broke. (In 1968, Medicare paid $303 for a cholecystectomy in Texas; Blue Shield paid $95, at most.)

Doctors who reined in their fees—like St. Louis internist Michael Karl—viewed the Medicare pirates with less than respect. "The issue divided the medical community," Karl says. "But Medicare sure made a lot of doctors rich."

It also changed doctor-patient relations. One internist had been treating a widow for nominal fees; she had customarily given him a quart of raspberries in gratitude. When Medicare arrived, so did a steady source of government dollars to pay for her care. "It's funny, but I don't feel nearly as interested in her care as I did," he wrote. "I feel as though I've lost a friend and gained a customer."

It wasn't long before doctors gained not only customers, but a strict overseer in the form of a cost-conscious Health Care Financing Administration. Lyndon Johnson had promised that Medicare wouldn't interfere with the practice of medicine. But what's a promise? Medicare has subjected doctors to utilization review, peer review panels, diagnosis-related groups, the resource-based relative value scale, self-referral bans, and, most recently, guidelines for documenting evaluation and management services.

"I think the AMA's opposition to Medicare in the early 1960s was the right decision at the time," says AMA trustee and gastroenterologist William Mahood. "Many of the things that we feared have come to pass."

However, Princeton University health economist Uwe Reinhardt says doctors ought to keep things in perspective. "The unbelievable spigot that government opened added enormous funds to doctors," says Reinhardt. "They should quit whining."

MANAGED CARE: THE FINAL INDIGNITY

By the early 1970s, the combination of third-party payers and fee-for-service medicine had helped ignite what lawmakers and business alike viewed as a health-care crisis. Because third parties footed most or all of the bill, once-conservative patients demanded more medical services. And doctors were more than happy to ratchet up their production.

The Nixon administration looked to health maintenance organizations as a way to curb spending as well as foster preventive care. The HMO of its dreams was Kaiser Permanente.

Kaiser's story began in California's Mojave Desert in 1933 during the construction of an aqueduct to satiate thirsty Los Angeles. The contractor's insurer hired a doctor named Sidney Garfield to care for the workers. Garfield, who advocated "the maintenance of health" and group practice, collected a nickel a day per worker from the insurer for treating job-related injuries. Employees chipped in another nickel a day for medical care not related to work.

Industrialist Henry Kaiser took this system to a higher level when he engaged Garfield to provide comprehensive, capitated medical services—first, to workers and dependents at his Grand Coulee Dam project in Washington and then, during World War II, at Kaiser's California shipyards. Garfield's people kept the workers healthy, attending even to the lunches they ate, and the workers welded ships at record rates.

In 1945, Kaiser opened a nonprofit health plan to the public. Though salaried Kaiser physicians were an affront to fee-for-service medicine for years, enrollment grew to 9.1 million by 1998. Kaiser Permanente was what Nixon had in mind when Congress passed a 1973 law subsidizing the development of HMOs. Growth was slow at first, with only 6 million Americans enrolled in HMOs in 1976. But healthcare inflation eventually drove American corporations—as well as Medicare and Medicaid—into the tight embrace of managed care. By 1996, 49.4 million Americans belonged to HMOs, with another 14.7 million in less restrictive point-of-service organizations, and yet another 96.1 million in preferred provider organizations, which amount to discounted fee-for-service on a leash.

Some doctors feel their profession needs managed care to shape it up, both financially and clinically. Economist Uwe Reinhardt agrees. "Physician autonomy has not guaranteed quality," he says. Nevertheless, managed care has set off the loudest howls about intrusiveness.

In 1997, 71 percent of physicians polled by the AMA said managed care was too involved in their decision-making. To many, the corporate medicine identified with managed care has fulfilled the dire predictions about national health insurance almost 60 years ago—an assembly line of patients treated by hired hands.

"It's not the government, but the business world that has taken over medicine," says internist Michael Karl. "The government would have been the lesser of two evils."

WILL MSAs RESTORE PHYSICIAN AUTONOMY?

So what choices do doctors have now? Some believe that if they control the payment mechanism (shades of the early Blue Shield plans!), they can preserve their autonomy. Consequently, doctors have formed their own HMOs and PPOs. But it's a risky business. The California Medical Association formed a PPO in 1995—and watched it file for bankruptcy last June.

Other doctors cultivate self-pay patients while picking third-party payers carefully. Washington, DC internists Bryan Arling and David Patterson, for example, shun managed-care plans.

"A third of our patients are self-pay," says Arling, who set up shop in 1977. "Many of them are going outside their insurance network. The other two-thirds have insurance that covers most or all of our fees, but the majority of them pay us before they leave the office.

"When the patient hands us a check, I become directly accountable to him. I like that. In fact, I feel blessed. I look forward to coming to work each day."

Wanting that blessedness for more doctors, the AMA recently endorsed switching from employer-based insurance to insurance chosen and owned by individuals. While remaining free to stick with their insurance at work, individuals would be allowed to opt for medical savings accounts or form cooperatives to buy coverage, funding it partly with employer contributions.

Such a move, argues AMA trustee William Mahood, would reduce the third-party intrusion rampant with employer-based insurance. "With our plan, the patient will be in the driver's seat," Mahood says, "and the doctor will be riding shotgun."

The AMA proposal would require rewriting tax and insurance laws to shift the incentives from employer-based insurance to individual-based insurance. Will Congress buy the AMA's idea? Can consumers fend for themselves in purchasing coverage? Will individual insurance wreck the employer-based market by draining off healthy people who need only modest coverage?

While those questions are sorted out, doctors must continue to live with checks—and challenges—from third-party payers.

2

Compensation Principles

KENNETH M. HEKMAN

INTRODUCTION

There is an old adage in medical group management circles about the three kinds of physician compensation formulas available: the one you used last year, the one you are using this year, and the one you will use next year. The adage speaks volumes about the controversy of compensation. It seems to be a topic of perpetual discontent in many groups. It highlights the shortcoming of mathematical models to symbolize human values. It is frequently cited as the cause for group practice divorces, although seldom is it lauded as the glue that holds a group together. It touches at the heart of the delicate trust relationships among physicians, but does so with the appearance of engineering precision. Compensation formulas are poorly designed tools to measure human values and trust, but the money has to be split somehow, and mathematical models at least can be shaped and modified by human values and trust. David Tenenbaum expressed wisdom with this observation: "Practice style, patient population (and payer mix) and resource expenses can vary wildly among physicians in any group practice. All affect the compensation plan—or at least how the physicians *feel* about the compensation plan."[1]

The feelings about physician compensation are almost *universally* intense—more so, it seems, than executive compensation in other industries. Top executives in companies large and small are often rewarded in a combination of ways. They receive a salary, and a bonus if the company is profitable; they may also receive stock options or become shareholders in an enterprise of growing value. That is usually not the case for physicians. Medical practices do not grow in value nearly to the degree that other businesses do. While executives benefit from deferred compensation in the form of stock value, physicians must depend on income for both current and long-term value. There is a lot at stake for physicians when it comes to deciding about compensation. Therefore, it should come as no surprise that distribution systems are hot topics at group practice board meetings.

It is remarkable, when we take a moment to reflect, how this noble profession is compensated. As a society, we pay those we entrust with the mysteries of life and health, for the most part, by a form of piecework, like factory workers. The public treats physicians like sales people who depend on a commission to support their families. It is a system that devalues the art of medicine and replaces it with a value for volume and for marketing. We expect quality, but we pay for production.

I have a friend who owns an auto body shop. He showed me the manual he uses to prepare estimates for his work. It detailed each part of every kind of car, and specified how long it should take to replace the part. Estimating, then, was a process of preparing an inventory of the parts that needed replacement, then multiplying an hourly rate by the number of work units assigned to each part. He knew what the market was for hourly rates, and he understood that his profitability would go up if he could "beat the clock"—complete the repair in less than the designated time. I was struck at the similarity between that parts manual and the Resource Based Relative Value System (RBRVS) established initially for Medicare reimbursement in the early '90s. Even the use of conversion factors (like hourly rates) seemed all too familiar. As his customer, I was hoping that he would not cut corners to save time while fixing my car. I expected quality. But my auto insurance company wanted the lowest bid. They were only willing to pay for production. The comparison was uncanny and unsettling. Are health insurance companies also looking for the lowest-cost methods of resolving health issues, without regard to the quality of care? Are people to be treated like cars? Has insurance made health care services a commodity like auto repairs?

The art and science of designing physician compensation systems have evolved rapidly. I believe the 1990s will be remembered as the decade of transition for physician compensation. Two important trends converged in the last decade of the millenium to set the stage for physician compensation in the next chapter of this fast-moving societal institution. First, managed care and its derivatives gathered steam in the '90s, bringing a critical mass to the driving force behind how doctors get paid. The Kaiser Family Foundation reports that the rise in managed care (including HMOs, PPOs and Point-of-Service or POS plans) has been dramatic, rising from 27 percent of employer-sponsored health plans in 1988 to 93 percent in 2001.[2] The rate of growth in HMO enrollments may be slowing, but physicians cannot ignore the impact of managed care policies and politics on their behavior and their economic welfare.[3] The system of rewards for keeping people healthy, rather than overwhelming them with technology and services when they are sick, is so antithetical to the former way of life that many have termed the duality schizophrenic.

The second trend, driven in part by the first, is the increasing popularity of medical groups. The American Medical Association reported that group physicians grew from 10.6 percent of the total non-federal physicians in 1965 to 34.4 percent by 1995.[4] They conclude that "there is a slow but steady trend toward the group practice of medicine." With this switch has come a host of considerations regarding physician compensation that solo physicians never had to deal with. Solo physicians had full and singular responsibility for their personal productivity and for managing their overhead. Physicians in groups share those responsibilities, and must find ways to collaborate to meet each other's needs. This interdependence is about as antithetical to independent-minded former solo physicians as managed care is to the familiar fee-for-service system.

At the apex of these two converging factors is collegiality, the ability to get along and persevere for the common good, even under trying circumstances. And at the heart of collegiality is the physician compensation system. The agreements doctors make with each other about how to divide the pie is the core subject of this book. Those agreements are symbolic of the trust and respect colleagues have for each other, the ring of their professional marriage. Compensation is the cornerstone of physician collegiality in medical group practices, and it requires the kind of orderly process and goal congruence, attention and respect due any foundational construct.

Physician compensation policies may also be at the heart of an efficient and effective national health care system. Compensation can become a powerful motivator, and designing physician incentives on a micro level may well have a macro impact, community by community. The introduction of Medicare in 1966 was a good demonstration of that. Physicians were rewarded for increasing the volume and complexity of their services, fueling double-digit health care inflation that has been the motivating force for reform movements ever since.

But I would like to think we are learning better ways to encourage physicians to be the caring servants we need them to be. Managed care has turned medicine on its head in many ways, leaving some health care services dizzy, while others find their balance and surf the landscape in ways that benefit patients and caregivers alike. A well designed compensation formula can honor the best of both groups' interests. Vasilios Kalogredis and Michael Burke perhaps said it best: "The formula you choose should engender goodwill among the partners and encourage everyone to work together to ensure that the total patient care being provided by the group is of the highest quality."[5]

I have often thought of money as a byproduct of service rather than an end in itself. That contention was affirmed by Earl Nightingale, the radio personality from the mid-1900s. In his epic audiotape series, "Lead the Field," Nightingale says, "Money is the harvest of our production. The amount of money we receive will always be in direct ratio to the demand for what we do, our ability to do it, and the difficulty of replacing us." In other words, our rewards will be in direct proportion to our service. While that may simplify a very complex topic, it points to the important truth that money is a byproduct of service rather than the other way around.

BASIC PRINCIPLES

We will examine three basic principles at work in designing and implementing sound compensation systems for medical groups, then share a bit of wisdom gained from experience. First, we will look at the importance of aligning incentives, then the role that information systems play, and finally the value of the design process.

Aligning Incentives

Susan Cejka, founder of Cejka and Associates, a physician recruitment and consulting firm, identifies three axioms of compensation in advising physicians and managers. First, she says people do what they are rewarded to do. If the incentive is to see lots of patients, then that is what doctors will do. If the incentives are to refer patients to specialists (as are capitated primary care physicians in a contract where specialists are also paid capitation), they'll refer quickly. Second, she points out that physicians are bright people, and they can unravel any system to determine how to make it benefit them (and they frequently do just that). Third, when designing a compensation system, you need to make sure the behaviors you reward are the ones you want. The consulting firm has tracked the evolution of pay plans with a survey of West Coast practices, showing that the shift in compensation plans has been rapid from a primary dependence first on production without capitation, to a dependence on straight salaries, to the emergence of a combination of productivity and incentive factors over the past decade.[6]

The alignment of incentives has two primary targets. A wise compensation formula is one that gives physicians some personal influence on their ability to increase production while they decrease overhead. There are many other factors that enter into a group's profitability picture that will be explored further in chapter 4, but these two are at the heart of determining how profitable a group will be. And they require interdependence to maximize the profit potential. Thus, a compensation formula functions like work rules might in a union contract. It lets everybody know what's expected individually and collectively, so the common welfare can be increased.

Feedback

Compensation systems depend on accurate and timely measurements. Physicians thrive on feedback to improve their clinical effectiveness. The same is true of their performance in other dimensions. For every incentive concept, there must be a valid method of measuring performance.

One of the fundamental tools that effective medical group administrators insist on is a monthly reporting system, one that goes beyond traditional financial statements to offer feedback on individual physicians' performance, using the measurements that correlate to their compensation formula. If physicians are to be rewarded for increasing the volume of services, then make sure they see how they are performing, month by month, in a combination of visits, procedures, relative value units (RVUs), charges or receipts. If the group and the individuals benefit by increasing the caseload of capitated patients, then show the enrollment figures on a monthly basis. The reports can gain value if they include comparisons to the prior year's experience or to budget-based targets, by performing variance analyses. Physicians respect data and usually respond to it systematically. They rely on research data to shape their medical judgments, and they are prone to look for comparative information to shape their production as well.

The emerging field of outcomes measurement is likely to become a vital part of compensation systems and feedback mechanisms in the future. We will explore that topic more in chapter ten, but it is valuable to note at this point that measurement systems need to stay one step ahead of compensation incentives. As clinical outcomes are tied to managed care reimbursement, administrators will want to introduce outcomes-related consequences to physician compensation.

The importance of accuracy in these reports speaks for itself. If these monthly feedback systems are to be relied upon to allow physicians to gauge their performance, they must find the reports consistently trustworthy. Excel™ spreadsheets or similar software products lend themselves well to developing easy-to-update monthly report formats. If a manager spends one hour per month preparing the reports, the return on investment for that time can be enormous.

The Delicate Balance

Many administrators view the struggle to find fair compensation for physicians to be an impossible task. In a sense they are right, because at its very core the process requires resolution of competing values. Physicians are quite naturally seeking to preserve their portion of the pie within a group. But their self-interest must compete with group interests. In essence, every group has to wrestle with basic beliefs about how important group effort is, compared to individual effort; how important the mission is of the organization, compared to its profitability or its margin; and how important work is, compared to taking care of one's family. Each of these values represents polarities, described more fully by Barry Johnson, PhD, author of *Polarity Management*.[7]

Polarities are interdependent opposites. They are values or forces that are competing for attention, but both are necessary for a healthy organization to advance its interests. For example, a group of physicians needs to pay attention both to the individual efforts of its members and to its group efforts—its organizational efforts—at streamlining the practice. Highly productive physicians who work in inefficient groups are likely to see their efforts compromised by high overhead or by internal conflicts that circumvent their individual efforts to provide services and to receive compensation. On the other hand, a group that pays more attention to preserving its relationships than it does to achieving production is also at risk of compromising its profitability and attraction to newcomers. So these two interests, the group effort and the individual effort, must be prioritized and balanced.

As administrators provide leadership to their groups in rewriting the physician compensation plan, they will inevitably encounter these discussions about values. In managing those discussions, and in managing those polarities, it will be important for the leadership team to listen carefully to both sides, to make sure that each value is given equal opportunity to express itself and to be appreciated. Until the positive contribution of each value is understood and the fears about its opposite are articulated, the organization may be at a standstill in devising a wise compensation system.

The Role of Benefits in the Compensation Picture

Most compensation discussions focus exclusively on the formula for determining W-2 compensation, but that's only part of the picture. To do an adequate job of benchmarking compensation, it would be imperative for medical group administrators to include a benchmark for the benefits as well. In our experience, the variance of commitment to deferred compensation (i.e., retirement plan contributions) varies dramatically from zero to 15 percent. Groups that want to maximize funding their retirement plans can set aside even more by including both federally qualified retirement plans and 401(k) programs in their benefit structure.

Compensation is, at least in part, a symbol of safety, and the benefit structure is an integral part of that safety foundation. If compensation is maximized, but benefits are compromised, even highly compensated physicians may feel like they are underpaid if they do not feel safe with their benefit structure.

One exercise that I find universally compelling is to develop a spreadsheet that articulates the exact dollar value of each benefit in addition to compensation. When physicians (and staff, for that matter,) see the total cost to the corporation of supporting their efforts, the stark realities serve as an important reminder of the truest picture, and help to put the decisions and discussions in a realistic context.

Correlating Compensation

While most consultants will heartily advise that compensation systems need to be aligned with the group's strategic directions, few have ways of measuring how well that alignment is actually taking place. One little-known method that can be particularly enlightening is to use the correlation coefficient function within an Excel spreadsheet. The correlation coefficient is a statistical method for identifying the relationship between two measurable factors. For example, it may be helpful to compare actual compensation with many of the factors of production mentioned in chapter 4, such as visits, net collections, the relative value units, or some other measure of productivity. If the group has a few years of data that allow them to track the effectiveness of their compensation policy, it may be extremely helpful to see how the factors of productivity they intended to use as rewards actually correlated with the end result of physician compensation. It is a statistically meaningful measurement of the realities of a complex dynamic.

The Value of the Process

A compensation formula is only as good as the process that designed it and the system that regulates it. A formula thrust upon physicians by an eager administrator has as much chance of succeeding as an ice cube in Phoenix. The formula must be a byproduct of the trust that builds over time among physicians. That is why merger consultants frequently suggest that the compensation formula be one of the last things to be designed as groups come together. It takes time for trust to build. History is either the friend or the enemy of trust, as we have seen in the development of European alliances and wars over the past century. Compensation systems are like the post-war agreements formed by the Allied forces (NATO) and the Axis (Warsaw Pact). They signal the conditions of a truce, the rules for cooperation, and the goals and rewards of collaboration, but trust comes from honoring the agreements over time.

So, too, the process of developing a compensation formula needs to be a democratic process. With smaller groups especially, consensus is critical. As groups grow larger, they may rely upon representative input, but all the interests must be represented, and a majority must rule if the system is to be successful. As with international agreements, not every partner will be completely comfortable with every provision of the agreement, but the overall good of the agreement must outweigh the risks of no agreement. Some have argued that the best sign of a good compensation formula is that everyone is "equally unhappy" with it.

If the design process is the mother of a wise compensation formula, implementation is its father. A well designed formula implemented poorly is just as sure to fail as a poorly designed formula. The concepts of aligned incentives must be the foundation of sound design, but if the group has no valid way of measuring the behaviors it wishes to incent, or if exceptions are made at every whimper of discontent, the compensation system will be compromised. It is important for the group to have methods for reviewing the results of their formula, and for modifying major inequities, but if the incentive concepts are sound and the measurement methods accurate, physicians should be willing to commit to live by their agreement, regardless of the impact on each individual.

WISDOM FROM EXPERIENCE

Perhaps it is presumptuous to expect that by reading a book, physicians and medical group administrators will be fully equipped to tailor a compensation system that fits the values, market dynamics and measurement capabilities of every medical practice. Compensation systems are dynamic. They must change as the group values change, as the market evolves, and as feedback capabilities are refined. The purpose of this section is to offer some perspectives about physician compensation, from years of observation in groups across the country, to temper the process.

1. **It all has to come from somewhere**.

   Every dollar that is to be distributed to physicians has a source. Physicians often regard certain dollars as being clearly attributable to their individual efforts, but that is almost never the case. In fact, every dollar that comes to the practice must flow because of a process that involves many people—patients, staff, insurers, hospitals, as well as physicians. If physicians expect to take out in compensation and benefits more than a fair share of their input, that money will have to come from somewhere else. It will either come from unsuspecting colleagues, from a benevolent employer (such as a hospital), or from illegal means.

This also means that physicians can't spend money they don't have direct control over. The tragedy is a common one. Physicians focus their attention on gross charges rather than net receipts, only to find that they don't have enough money in the bank to pay all the bills. Others borrow working capital rather than build up an appropriate reserve, only to find that they are under pressure to perform this year to pay for last year's capital improvements.

Sound compensation systems, then, must be integrated with financial discipline at both organizational and individual levels. A colleague who takes liberties with the time-off policy, or who wastes overhead resources, is actually taking something from his partners without their permission. Every dollar comes from somewhere.

2. **Collegiality grows with common goals and rewards.**

A sound compensation system cannot make a contentious group collegial, but it can make a collegial group more so. Trust breeds trust, and one of the best indicators of a sound compensation system is low physician turnover. If the system works as it is designed to work, rewarding the kinds of behaviors that satisfy the aspirations of both the group and most of the individual physicians, the participants find little reason to become discontented.

This is another indicator of why compensation systems are foundational to organizational stability and growth. An organization gains a strategic market advantage when it demonstrates stability. Patients gain confidence in a group that doesn't seem like a revolving door for medical staff. Insurers may be more willing to negotiate with a stable and growing medical group. Hospital executives are forced to respect the physicians who are pillars of the medical community. And all these strategic benefits derive, at least partly, from a sound compensation system.

3. **Simple is better.**

Simple elegance is striking in architecture, nature and the arts. But it also has significant value when it comes to designing a physician compensation system. I have seen more than my share of formulas that seem to have been put together by a committee where everyone had to have their imprint on it with a minimum of compromise. The result is an unwieldy composite of concepts that are difficult or impossible to measure accurately, that no one can explain in a few sentences, and that ends up being a target for contention rather than a treaty for peace. If physicians have difficulty deciphering the impact of their behaviors on their incomes, how can the formula be expected to reward the intended incentives?

The Winchester House in San Jose, California, is a model of complexity. The heiress to the firearms fortune reportedly believed that her life would continue as long as construction continued at her mansion. The result is a convoluted menagerie of stairways that go nowhere, rooms with no purpose, and a mysterious aura. The same can become true of physician compensation systems that get tweaked into meaninglessness. It takes discipline to remain simple, as Abraham Lincoln discovered with multiple drafts of his Gettysburg Address. But the impact of his six-minute speech echoes to this day as a model of the benefits of simplicity, among other things.

Kurt Mosley, vice president of marketing, Merritt Hawkins and Associates, Irving, Texas, describes the value of simplicity. "Compensation models can vary widely depending on the reimbursement methods used, but two qualifications must be present for the model to be effective: it must be easy to understand and it must be equitable. If the model is not easy to understand, it only breeds mistrust throughout the organization because no one knows how others are being compensated or if they are being compensated fairly."[8]

I would challenge administrators to provide a one-page narrative description of their compensation plan to show their prospective physician recruits, along with a spreadsheet that models how the formula works. If you can explain it in a few paragraphs, highlighting which behaviors are rewarded and why, with a demonstration of how the numbers play out in a typical fashion, you have a much higher opportunity of helping physicians succeed within the group. An example is Pediatric Associates, P.C., shown at the end of this chapter.

4. **Don't try to solve every organizational problem with the compensation formula**.

Compensation formulas can be powerful motivators, but they also have limitations. It is a poor tool for adjusting the behavior of a physician who performs immorally. It will not stop the obsessive progress-note-writer from wasting his/her and everyone else's time. By itself, it will not punish the doctor who is consistently rude with patients and staff. A physician who is independently wealthy and satisfied is not likely to find profit-building motives fulfilling.

Compensation systems are for deciding how to distribute the pie, but they are insufficient as managers of physician behavior. Physicians and managers still need to hold each other accountable for collaborative behaviors, whether they translate directly to profits or not. If an amendment to a compensation formula is proposed to correct unwanted behavior from one or two physicians in a twenty-doctor group, it is likely to be ineffective. It may even end up punishing the innocent, while the guilty physicians go unscathed.

Counterproductive behaviors of a few aberrant physicians must be addressed by peer reviews, management pressure, and basic communication. Let management be management, and let compensation systems be compensation systems. They should be intertwined, but not confused for each other.

Conclusion

Designing and implementing physician compensation systems is an art form. In the remaining chapters, you will see a variety of approaches to that art, each with a unique perspective on how physicians can form their peace agreements. Enjoy the book as you might enjoy an art museum or concert. Savor the insights and tones, and blend them with your own to create a harmonious result for your medical group.

EXAMPLE

Pediatric Associates, P.C.

Physicians at Pediatric Associates, P.C. have the opportunity to be compensated at above-market levels by working diligently and wisely in managing patient care. The practice has a long history of service in the area, and a reputation for clinical excellence that consistently attracts patients in good standing. This compensation plan outlines the principles and tactics designed to balance physicians' interests with patients' interests, and to reward physicians who adhere to the incentives that are integral to wise and prudent patient care.

General Principles of the Compensation Plan

Physicians at PAPC are rewarded individually for:

- Accessibility for timely service to loyal patients;
- Efficient management of patients under capitation contracts;
- Procedural intensity for fee-for-service patients; and
- High volumes of patient fee-for-service visits.

As a group, the practice is rewarded for:

- Maintaining overhead efficiency;
- Attracting and retaining physicians to match the facility's capacity;
- Supporting each other with call responsibilities and shared governance;
- Attracting and retaining competent and compassionate support staff;
- Deploying non-physician providers in effective and efficient ways; and
- Remaining open to sound market expansion.

Specific Components of the Compensation Plan

1. Compensation for newly recruited physicians is initially assured by a salary guarantee from the local recruiting hospital. PAPC will extend that guarantee as a threshold of support for up to five years from the date of employment at the rate of $120,000 annually.

2. Revenues and expenses for shareholders are calculated according to the three-part compensation worksheet shown below.

Revenue principles include the following:

- Fee-for-service receipts are attributed individually;
- Capitation receipts are allocated as a percent of individual capitation charges of all providers;
- Excess of revenues over expenses from non-shareholder providers are distributed equally among shareholders;
- Physician incentive payments, risk and case management receipts are attributed individually; and
- Revenue totals are adjusted by buy-in agreements as may be required.

Expense principles include the following:

- Total overhead costs are distributed 60% fixed, 40% variable; and
- The variable portion of overhead is distributed by net professional charges (NPC).

PAPC Spreadsheet 1

	Dr. A	Dr. B	Dr. C	Total
Days in office per year	140.5	141.5	150.0	432.0
Visits	3,262	2,665	2,924	8,851
Net professional charges	$290,061	$277,072	$357,802	$924,935
Charges per day	$2,064	$1,958	$2,385	
Visits/day	23	19	19	
NPC/visit	$89	$104	$122	

Revenues

	Dr. A	Dr. B	Dr. C	Total
FFS receipts	$194,959	$181,429	$236,303	$612,691
Distributed capitation receipts from Spreadsheet 2	$135,602	$115,555	$127,623	$378,780
Net other profit shared equally from Spreadsheet 3	$130,956	$130,956	$130,956	$392,867
HMO incentive receipts	$38,515	$28,765	$7,083	$74,363
Risk Receipts	$54,657	$7,710	$12,446	$74,813
Other payback	$6,014	$6,014	$1,526	$13,554
Case mgmt.	$1,213	$1,044	$372	$2,629
Dr. C buy-in	$2,502	$2,502	−$5,004	$0
Total receipts	$564,418	$473,975	$511,305	$1,549,697

Expenses

		Dr. A	Dr. B	Dr. C	Total
Total Overhead					$1,070,764
Fixed Costs	60%				$642,458
Variable Costs	40%				$428,306
Fixed costs per shareholder		$214,153	$214,153	$214,153	$642,458
Variable costs distributed by NPC		$134,317	$128,303	$165,686	$428,306
Retained profit		$4,200	$4,200	$4,200	
Total costs		$352,670	$346,655	$384,039	
Profit		**$211,748**	**$127,319**	**$127,266**	**$466,333**
Individual costs		($21,318)	($14,387)	($8,414)	
Distributable profit		$190,430	$112,932	$118,852	
Salary taken		($126,269)	($107,568)	($86,383)	
PIP taken		($20,000)	($9,568)	($7,083)	
Net distributable profit		$44,161	($4,204)	$25,386	$65,343

Validity Tests

	Dr. A	Dr. B	Dr. C	Total
Comp as % of total receipts	34%	24%	23%	27%
Contribution to overhead	$352,670	$346,655	$384,039	$1,083,364
Overhead as % of net receipts	62%	73%	75%	70%

Summary

	Dr. A	Dr. B	Dr. C	Total
Receipts	$564,418	$473,975	$511,305	$1,549,697
Overhead	$352,670	$346,655	$384,039	$1,083,364
Compensation	$190,430	$112,932	$118,852	$422,214

PAPC Spreadsheet 2

	Dr. A	Dr. B	Dr. C	All other	Total
Cap charges	$79,194	$60,285	$71,668	$215,263	$426,410
Percent	19%	14%	17%	50%	
Cap receipts					$452,072
Allocated by % of Cap Charges	$83,960	$63,913	$75,981	$228,218	$452,072
Former Doctor's Cap Receipts				($73,292)	
Leftover—Nurse practitioner (NP) Cap Receipts				$154,926	
NP Cap Allocation equally	$51,642	$51,642	$51,642	$154,926	
Total cap receipts allocated	$135,602	$115,555	$127,623	$378,780	

PAPC Spreadsheet 3

Revenues

	Dr. D	NP 1	NP 2	NP 3	NP 4	NP 5	All Others	Total
FFS receipts	$99,432	$141,017	$139,321	$119,830	$14,838	$16,948	$16,984	$548,370
Capitation/risk receipts	$88,342							$88,342
HMO incentive (less staff bonuses)	$20,578							$20,578
Total revenues	$208,352	$141,017	$139,321	$119,830	$14,838	$16,948	$16,984	$657,290
Expenses								
Direct salary	$41,218	$46,334	$40,377	$39,808	$10,600	$0	$0	$178,337
Direct benefits								
HMO Incentive/Risk	$38,729							
Deferred Compensation	$23,569							
Staff Bonuses	$574							
Payroll taxes—10% of salary		$4,633	$4,038	$3,981				
Dues		$265	$340	$270	$200			
Meetings		$1,041	$0	$1,460				
Malpractice insurance		$371	$371	$371	$1,373			
Malpractice insurance Refund		($559)	($150)	($67)				
Health insurance		$0	$1,362	$0	$1,604			
401K match		$1,095	$952	$263				
Total expenses	$104,090	$53,180	$47,290	$46,085	$10,800	$2,977	$0	$264,423
Net Contribution to Overhead	$104,262	$87,837	$92,031	$73,745	$4,038	$13,971	$16,984	$392,867

Legal Aspects of Physician Compensation

KENNETH G. HOFMAN, JD

INTRODUCTION

Where is Norman Rockwell when we need him? Through his art, Mr. Rockwell cultivated an image of physicians as caring allies of their patients. The only hint of cynicism that Rockwell ever portrayed was a young boy momentarily studying the credentials hanging on the wall of his physician's office.

Welcome to the new world, where no physician is immune from criticism. While most patients may give high marks to their personal physician, public cynicism for the profession as a whole is on the rise. A sound conclusion is that this cynicism is a result of the manner in which the federal government has come to view doctors. From the myriad of laws and regulations governing physicians, to the public statements of government officials at the highest levels, a distinctly non-Rockwellian image appears. In fact, the image resembles the gun-slinging con man from the Wild West far more than it resembles an elderly teddy bear of a man checking the vitals of a young female patient's doll.

Just visit the government's Web sites that are dedicated to "Fighting Fraud and Abuse." You will learn that the government's clear premise is that fraud and abuse are rampant. The result of this premise has been a series of legislative and regulatory initiatives aimed at reducing fraudulent billing activities. The resulting difficulty is that even the most well-intentioned medical provider is frustrated in his or her attempts to comply with laws which are difficult to understand and to apply.

The impact is felt in the area of physician compensation, which was historically considered a physician's private business. Not anymore. The laws now even intrude into the confidential agreements within a group practice regarding the manner in which net income is distributed.

This chapter is intended to provide you with some insights into the basic themes of these laws and to attempt to provide you with some guidance in addressing compensation issues. I will first summarize the most important and relevant federal statutes in this area, and then apply the law to physician compensation concepts.

Please note that my discussion is hardly definitive. First, my discussion is not legal advice, and you need to consult with qualified attorneys who practice in the health care arena, regarding your particular circumstances. Second, the law is not definitive. At best, the law can only be described as "emerging." A health care attorney never gets the opportunity to say to a client, "The answer is clear, and you are *completely* safe."

THE LAW

The purpose of this chapter is to introduce you to the basics, so that you can spot issues in structuring new relationships and defining the economic consequences of the relationship among the parties. This summary is limited to the basic federal statutes that govern health care providers. You need to be aware that each state has its own legislative initiatives that impact health providers, including their compensation arrangements. With that disclaimer in mind, we now turn to federal law.

The Fraud and Abuse Act

In addition to the Federal False Claims Act, fraud and abuse regulation has been the federal government's primary resource to address fraudulent billing practices. In summary, the regulations prohibit the payment or receipt of "remuneration" paid to induce referrals of patients whose care may be reimbursed through Medicare or Medicaid. That seems quite straightforward. It should prevent the following type of illegal conduct:

X is a drug manufacturer's representative. X goes to physician A and says, "I know my product is higher priced than the generic. Prescribe my brand, and we will pay you 5 percent of retail price." That is a kickback, and it is illegal.

The difficulty arises because the federal government has attempted to apply the Fraud and Abuse Act to many different situations, from waivers of co-payments and deductibles to the manner in which incentive compensation is calculated. Additionally, in limited cases construing the regulations, courts have shown a willingness to apply them to circumstances well beyond the narrow "kickback" setting which we all agree is illegal.

Due to the hue and cry of health care attorneys and lobbyists, the Office of the Inspector General (OIG), which is charged with enforcing the regulations, has formulated certain safe harbors. The following are particularly relevant.

Personal Services and Management Agreements

An agreement calling for payments from a principal to an agent for personal services should not violate the Act if the parties enter into a written agreement that (1) lasts for at least one year; (2) specifies the services which the agent will provide to the principal; (3) provides compensation that is truly the fair market value for those services; and (4) meets certain other criteria. This safe harbor is helpful for independent contractor relationships between a physician or a physician group and any persons or entities who pay for medical services, including payors and hospitals.

Bonafide Employees

Payments made by an employer to an employee under the terms of a bonafide employment relationship should not be found to violate the fraud and abuse regulations. The term "employee" is defined in the same manner as it is under the Internal Revenue Code. Consequently, items like the "20 factor test," which the IRS has announced to distinguish between employees and independent contractors, also apply to determine whether this safe harbor may apply.

While the bonafide employee safe harbor appears to be very broad on its face, the OIG may still challenge an employment arrangement where compensation is being paid for referrals. An example could be where a physician sells his or her practice to another provider, such as a hospital. The hospital pays a relatively meager amount for the assets of the practice to avoid an argument that the hospital is paying for future referrals of patients. Instead, the hospital pays the physician a large sum of money under an employment agreement. The safe harbor likely may not apply, because the OIG would argue that the hospital is indirectly purchasing a stream of referrals from the physician through inflation of compensation.

The Stark Laws

The Stark laws are named for Fortney "Pete" Stark, the former chair of the House Ways and Means Subcommittee on Health Financing. While perhaps well intentioned, the Stark laws are perhaps even more pervasive and confusing than the fraud and abuse regulations.

In summary, the Stark laws provide that, if a physician has a financial relationship with an entity, then the physician may not make a referral to that entity for the purpose of providing certain designated health services for which payment may be made under Medicare or Medicaid. The designated health services are divided into 11 different categories, ranging from clinical laboratory services to inpatient and outpatient hospital services. The financial relationships include either an ownership or investment interest or a compensation arrangement. In addition, referrals include the transfer of a patient within a physician's own office.

Like the fraud and abuse regulations, the Stark laws are designed to prevent truly unethical behavior. For example, assume that a community has 10 primary care doctors who get together to start a clinical laboratory and charge significantly more for lab services than the local hospital. Each of the 10 physicians refers his or her patients to the captive lab, in spite of the blatant conflict of interest. We all agree that such an arrangement is contrary to public policy and is unethical.

However, the government applies the Stark laws to a much broader range of activities than simply the kind this illustration represents. To provide some guidance to physicians, the Stark laws and accompanying regulations have enacted certain exceptions to the Stark laws that are similar to the fraud and abuse safe harbors. An important difference between the Stark exceptions and the fraud and abuse safe harbors is that conduct that falls outside of a fraud and abuse safe harbor is not necessarily in violation of the fraud and abuse regulations, while behavior which falls outside of a Stark exception is considered to be illegal.

Some Stark exceptions that apply to compensation arrangements include the following.

Physician Services

Under the Stark laws, a physician may have a compensation relationship with another entity or physician to whom the physician may make referrals, but only if that physician, or another physician member of the same group practice, performs the services. This Stark exception means that physicians who are members of the same group practice may make referrals to one another without violating the Stark laws. However, this exception is conditioned upon meeting the definition of a group practice. This definition is very involved, and has several requirements, including that each physician perform substantially all of his/her services through the group and through the joint use of shared office space and personnel. In addition, the group cannot pay a physician in the group for referrals that he or she may make to another physician in the group.

In-Office Ancillary Services

Physicians typically will be reimbursed for services that they perform personally or those that others perform, but that are "incident to" the services of the physician. Consequently, the Stark regulations outline an exception for "in-office ancillary services." No other Stark exception has received so much attention, or has been the subject of more discussion than this one. To meet this exception, the physicians must not only qualify as a "group practice," but must satisfy a number of other requirements that are similar to the "incident to" rules that govern physician billing. In other words, the physician must supervise the ancillary services directly from a common location, and bill collectively with the other group physicians.

Bonafide Employment Relationships

It is legal for an employer to pay an employed physician compensation if the arrangement meets factors that are very similar to the corresponding safe harbor to the fraud and abuse regulations. Again, the emphasis is upon the fair market value of the services being provided.

Personal Service Arrangements

The Stark laws also have an exception for independent contractor relationships, which closely resembles the fraud and abuse safe harbor.

Private Inurement

The third significant federal legal principle impacting physician compensation is private inurement, a concept that applies only to tax-exempt entities. Hospitals employ or otherwise contract with many physicians, and most hospitals are tax-exempt entities. Consequently, a basic understanding of private inurement principles is necessary for any physician contracting with hospitals or other tax-exempt entities.

The overriding principle in this area is that entities that are exempt from federal taxation under Section 501(c)(3) of the Internal Revenue Code must be organized for a public, rather than a private, benefit. A "public" benefit does not mean that the benefit needs to be directed to a governmental unit. Instead, the religious, charitable or educational purpose of the organization must flow to the organization's community generally, as opposed to flowing to a narrow group of individuals. Consistent with this concept of "no private benefit," a tax-exempt entity may not allow its net earnings or other charitable assets to "inure" to the benefit of any private individual or group of individuals. The tax regulations define these individuals as any person having a personal and private interest in the organization's activities. These individuals are often referred to as "insiders." In other words, hospitals may not direct a benefit to insiders.

The IRS generally attempts to take the position that employed and staff physicians are insiders. This issue is not settled. A far more reasonable conclusion would be to treat employed or staff physicians as insiders only when those physicians are in a position to have an impact on the hospital's decision-making, whether by virtue of administrative responsibilities, board membership or referral patterns.

One area that the IRS has reviewed closely in audits of hospitals is incentive compensation to employed physicians. The IRS has stated that incentive compensation arrangements should analyze the following five factors:

1. The employee receiving the compensation should have no participation in the management or control of the hospital, and the relationship must be completely at arm's length.

2. Incentive payments should serve a real and ascertainable business purpose completely independent of the benefit to the employee.

3. The amount of the compensation should be dependent upon the employee's meeting objectives, and should not be dependent upon incoming revenue of the hospital.

4. In addition to the written agreement, a review of the actual relationship should reveal no evidence of additional benefits, and hospital policy should exist to prevent "off-agreement" benefits.

5. The hospital should impose a "ceiling" on the compensation to the physician, to avoid any possibility of a windfall to the physician.

Where the IRS finds private inurement, the issue then becomes "What is the penalty?" The harshest option is that the IRS can attempt to revoke the entity's tax-exempt status. This is a catastrophic result that causes hospital income to be taxable, donations from individuals to be non-deductible, and tax-exempt bonds to become taxable.

In an attempt to stiffly penalize offending organizations without revoking their tax-exempt status, Congress included "intermediate sanctions" provisions under the terms of the Taxpayer Bill of Rights II legislation of 1996. Under the intermediate sanctions terminology, a tax-exempt entity cannot pay an "excess benefit" to a "disqualified person." If the entity enters into an "excess benefit transaction" the resulting penalty tax is 25 percent of the excess benefit, and a second tax of 200 percent of the excess benefit if the matter is not corrected prior to the IRS's formal assessment. The IRS can also pursue "organization managers" who participate in the excess benefit transaction, for 10 percent of the excess benefit up to a maximum of $10,000 per transaction. In other words, a hospital may emerge from an audit with its tax-exempt status intact, but the individuals receiving the "excess benefit" will not only need to return the excess benefit, but also pay the resulting penalties. Hospital managers may end up paying penalties from their personal assets.

As some protection from the intermediate sanctions, the IRS announced a procedure to establish a "rebuttable presumption of fair market value." By following this procedure, health providers can shift the burden of proof to the IRS to establish that a transaction is *not* at fair market value. Otherwise, the burden of proof is on the health provider to demonstrate that the transaction reflected fair market value.

To establish the rebuttable presumption, the health provider must follow the following five steps:

1. The transaction must be reviewed in advance, before the transaction is finalized.

2. The board of directors of the hospital, or a designated committee, all the members of which must be disinterested, must review the transaction to determine if the financial terms reflect fair market value.

3. The review must be based upon comparable data, typically generated by an outside party such a valuation consultant.

4. The board must base its determination on the comparable data.

5. All decisions relating to the transaction must be documented in the minutes, including a description of any rationale that supports a value higher than the comparable data that the consultant may have generated.

APPLYING THE LAW

The question then becomes, "What does this mean for me?" I will break down this discussion between group practice issues and hospital-physician contracting issues.

Group Practice Compensation Issues

I work with a number of physician practices, some of which have adopted rather complex methodologies for calculating compensation to their physician/employees. Still, almost all compensation models boil down to three basic steps: (1) The practice establishes a method for calculating the production that each individual physician generates; (2) The practice adopts a formula for determining the overhead that each physician consumes; (3) The overhead is offset against the production to determine the net distributable income that the practice pays to the physician/employee.

Based upon the analysis outlined above, one may question whether these compensation themes run afoul of the law. Physician practices need to know when they can pay productivity-based bonuses to their physicians.

The first piece of good news is that private inurement concepts do not apply to the private practice setting. As long as the physician group is organized as a for-profit entity under state law, the group need not worry about public benefit versus private inurement.

The fraud and abuse regulations and the Stark laws still apply. To address these laws, the group practice should attempt to fit within the fraud and abuse safe harbors and the Stark exceptions. The medical practice should have a written employment agreement with its physicians that describe the services the physicians will perform on behalf of the practice. The compensation methodology should be spelled out in the agreement, or in compensation policies adopted by the board of directors. The manner in which any incentive compensation is calculated must not include any consideration of referrals of an individual physician to his or her practice. Lastly, the overall compensation must be "commercially reasonable," even if the individual did not make any referrals to the practice.

Under these guidelines, most incentive compensation arrangements should not be in violation of the Fraud and Abuse Act or Stark laws. My experience has been that most practices do not give any "extra credit" to any physician in a practice based upon the number of referrals the physician makes to the practice. Instead, the physician's compensation is a product of the revenues the physician generates directly through patient visits or procedures. However, some practices allocate "points." For example, a group may decide that physician A gets one point for seeing a patient, but physician B gets one point because "she's my patient." Such a practice may be in violation of the Fraud and Abuse Act and Stark laws as compensation for referrals within the practice.

In terms of what constitutes "commercially reasonable" compensation, a practice should consider establishing a relationship with a consulting firm that can analyze compensation ranges in the region in which the group practices. By generating comparable market data, a group then has a basis upon which to conclude whether compensation is commercially reasonable. This does not mean that a group may not pay its physicians more than any other similarly situated group practice. Instead, the group should base its compensation determinations upon "referral-neutral" factors such as "our doctors have higher case loads than the doctors in the other practices."

In the last several years, group practices have begun to expand the scope of their contracting from internal employment arrangements to external independent contractor arrangements. For example, the number of written independent contractor agreements between hospitals and physician groups has increased significantly. The resulting issue is whether the physician group may accept incentive-based compensation from an entity that is not an employer.

As in the employment analysis, the group practice should attempt to fit these arrangements within the Fraud and Abuse safe harbors and Stark exceptions, but for personal services and management agreements. To qualify, the agreements must be in writing, must specify the services to be provided, must be signed by the parties and must be for at least one year. Most importantly, compensation must represent fair value, whether on a full-time or sporadic basis, and cannot take into consideration the value of referrals. Lastly, the agreement cannot include counseling or the promotion of a business arrangement that violates law.

Like bonafide employment relationships, many independent contractor agreements may fall within the terms of the safe harbor and the exception. Others may not. For example, an incentive compensation structure that increases based upon the number of patients whom the physician treats at a contracting facility will be suspect. However, a flat, per-unit compensation structure that reflects fair value should not violate the Act. Also, a predetermined annual amount that a facility pays to a physician group, regardless of the number of procedures actually performed during the year, may be legal as long as the annual amount is the result of calculating a reasonable estimate of the number of procedures *likely* to be performed, and not based upon an unrealistically large estimate of the number of procedures that will be performed during the year.

The examples outlined here are obviously far from all-encompassing. The marketplace is generating new and creative manners to compensate physicians for services performed. To evaluate each of these structures, physician groups need to rely upon legal counsel and perhaps outside consultants. While the Fraud and Abuse safe harbors and Stark exceptions are helpful, many contracting circumstances may fall within the zone that the government believes is illegal. Qualified legal counsel can assist in structuring contracts to help minimize this risk.

Another area that may be compensation-related and that involves physicians in private practice is ownership in other entities. Each practice should require each of its physicians to regularly disclose any ownership interest that he or she may have in another company that may be a vendor to the practice or a referral source to or from the practice. The government may argue that the ownership interest becomes the basis for determining to which location or entity a patient is referred, rather than the best interest of the patient and the interest of the government in cost-containment. The resulting problem is that the Fraud and Abuse safe harbors and Stark exceptions for ownership interests of this nature are very narrow. Consequently, practices should take care in structuring ownership interests in other entities.

Hospital-Compensated Physicians

As mentioned above, many physicians are contracting with tax-exempt entities, including hospitals. Unlike the good news of the last section, the bad news in this section is that private inurement concepts do apply. To reiterate from above, the person or group receiving an "excess benefit transaction" must not only return the benefit, but also must pay resulting penalties.

Still, the stakes to the hospital are even higher, because its tax-exempt status hangs in the balance. In addition, volunteer members of the hospital's board of directors could be sanctioned as "managers," and could be financially penalized even though they received no benefit from the transaction whatsoever. The result often is that legal counsel to the hospital advises a very conservative contracting approach, to avoid an appearance of impropriety. Legal counsel to the group often may urge a mildly more aggressive contracting approach that the attorney suggests is consistent with market conditions. The hospital rejects many of these proposals at the advice of its legal counsel because it is the safer approach. Where the hospital has contracting leverage, physicians may end up receiving less for their services than was true historically.

In other communities, the reverse can be true, with potentially catastrophic results to the hospital. For example, assume that a primary care physician practice attempts to utilize the fact that it admits many patients to a community hospital to negotiate more aggressive compensation arrangements. If that hospital is unwilling to walk that close to the legal fire, the physician practice may turn to the hospital in the adjacent community to "sell" its loyalty to the competitor. The winner (and ultimately, perhaps loser) is the hospital that may be most willing to expose itself to legal risks. The physician group may be unwittingly electing to obtain a short-term financial benefit, but ultimately may experience deferred penalties at the hand of the IRS, the OIG or the Department of Justice. These penalties can include being disqualified from participation under Medicare or Medicaid.

It is in these environments that the need for accurate valuation information becomes essential. The theme that runs through the Fraud and Abuse safe harbors and the Stark exceptions is "fair value." Also, the procedures that the IRS has announced to obtain the rebuttable presumption for intermediate sanctions purposes are also a sound methodology for fraud and abuse regulations and Stark law purposes.

For every personal service relationship with a tax-exempt hospital, the contracting physician group should work with the hospital to obtain a qualified valuation analysis for services of the type for which the hospital is contracting. The valuation report typically comes back showing a range that the analysis suggests represents fair value. If the compensation for the proposed services falls within the range, the hospital and the group both have some assurance that the arrangement is presumably legal. Where the compensation for the proposed services falls outside of the valuation range of the report, then the hospital and the group should articulate explicitly the manner in which the proposed services differ from those being performed in the marketplace. For example, has sufficient time passed since the time period when the comparative contracts were signed such that cost of living should be a factor? Are the physicians in the contracting group performing a greater range of services than those that are being performed at comparable locations? Do the physicians in the practice have a greater level of experience or clinical capabilities that warrant an increase in compensation? Whatever the rationale, it should be reflected in writing in the hospital's minutes and in the "statement of facts" section of the resulting contract.

Circumstances that the government has successfully challenged include the following:

1. Joint ventures where the resulting net income stream of the joint venture is disproportionately directed to a physician group.

2. Compensation for services that require no or little effort from the physicians. Let's use EKG over-reads as an example. Many hospitals have purchased the technology to have a computer-generated initial over-read to determine whether the EKG falls within certain parameters. A contracting physician group then over-reads only those

EKG reports that fall outside the parameters. Where compensation continues to be based upon the historical practice of over-reading every EKG, the hospital and physician group are running a risk. Some reduction in the compensation is warranted, given the reduction in services.

3. Bonus or incentive compensation arrangements that are tied to a percentage of a facility's revenues.

Special Hospital-Contracting Circumstances

Two particular areas involving hospital contracting have been the subject of concern to the government. The first is the acquisition of physician practices, and the second is recruitment incentives for physicians. Each of these two categories is an extension of the general category of hospital contracting, but the government has provided some specific guidance in each of these areas.

In the context of physician practices acquisition, the government is concerned that the hospital is using exempt assets to purchase a stream of referrals from the selling physician group that results in a "private benefit" to the physician group. Most of these transactions are a sale of assets from the practice group to the hospital. Problematic areas include a purchase price based upon a very aggressive overall asset evaluation, or a purchase price that reflects a large goodwill value. The government has argued that the payments then reflect consideration for future referrals.

The fraud and abuse regulations do have a safe harbor that applies to practice acquisitions, but it is very narrow. Under this safe harbor, the payment from one provider to another does not violate the fraud and abuse regulations if the entire transaction is completed within one year, and at the conclusion of that year, the selling practitioner is not in a position to make referrals to, or otherwise generate business for, the purchasing provider.

The Stark law contains an exception for "isolated transactions." Under this exception, a one-time sale of assets of a practice is not in violation of the Stark laws if (1) the purchase price is consistent with fair market value, and is not determined in a manner that takes into account, directly or indirectly, the volume or value of any referrals of any referring physician; (2) the transaction would be commercially reasonable even if no referrals were made by the selling provider; and (3) there are no additional transactions between the parties for six months after the conclusion of the transaction.

Fair value is again the cornerstone for determining legality. While most transactions are outside the fraud and abuse safe harbor, a purchase of assets from a physician may still be legal if the purchase price is based upon the fair market value for the assets. However, these transactions should always be properly documented and based upon a legitimate appraisal.

The second area of governmental intrigue is physician recruitment packages. These issues have arisen where hospitals have offered incentives to attract physicians to the community where the hospital is located. The issue becomes whether the hospital is paying to obtain the loyalty of the physician for future referrals or to benefit the community through the accessibility of a qualified new physician.

The IRS has taken a special interest in recruiting arrangements. Some of the basic principles that have emerged from the IRS include the following:

1. Incentives may not be used to retain a physician who is currently practicing in the community.

2. A hospital may only offer incentives based upon a documented community need for services of the type that the physician provides.

3. The hospital may not condition payment of any incentives upon a written or oral agreement that the physician will refer patients to the hospital in the future. The hospital may insist that the physician move to the community and establish a practice in the community, but cannot demand any extra services of loyalty from the physician.

4. A hospital may provide loans or guarantees of compensation, but only if the loans or the guarantees are evidenced by an executed promissory note that is adequately secured and leaving interest at a reasonable rate. Any forgiveness of the indebtedness must be conditioned upon the physician's remaining in the community for a period of not less than four years. Any income guarantees cannot exceed a period of two years, and the hospital may not provide any "off-agreement benefits."

CONCLUSION

The law governing physician compensation is emerging and complex. The government has provided some guidance to physicians who attempt to comply with the fraud and abuse regulations, the Stark law and the Private Inurement Prohibition for tax-exempt organizations. The common theme that emerges throughout is that compensation to physicians must reflect fair value, and cannot take into consideration the value of referrals that a physician makes to another physician or hospital provider. Physicians must take special pains to structure their compensation arrangements and relationships to attempt to avoid problems of this sort.

4

Fee for Service Models

KENNETH M. HEKMAN

INTRODUCTION

We have already seen in chapter 2 how managed care (HMOs, PPOs and POS plans) has come to dominate the health insurance industry formerly characterized by indemnity plans. But while indemnity plans and their fee-for-service reimbursement model have diminished nationally, twelve states have maintained less than 10 percent managed care penetration.[9] Likewise, managed care plans have also evolved to the point that many of them have come to look a lot like the old fee-for-service models. Thus, a kind of creative tension has arisen between these two fundamentally different methods of payment, such that the concepts of rewarding physicians on a per-service basis are likely to remain relevant. In this chapter, we'll examine some of the components of traditional fee-for-service compensation models, and consider how those components have an impact on compensation, even when indemnity plans and managed care plans are functioning side by side. Medical managers need to understand both concepts well to design and implement sound compensation plans.

GRAND FORMULA

If there is a simplified, over-arching formula for understanding compensation under fee-for service, it might look like this:

Formula for Success under Fee-for-Service

$$\$ = \text{Volume}_{encounters} \times \text{Intensity}$$

THE FACTORS OF PRODUCTION

Compensation policies are critical to the success of group practices, but they should also be understood in context. Policies aren't the only factor in determining how each member is paid. There are a variety of factors, including some outside the group's direct control, that influence the size of the distributable pie as much as or more than internal agreements. Let's examine a few of these important factors.

Fee Schedules

Standard professional fees mean far less in the current market than they did a few decades ago, but it is still true that reimbursement will not exceed what physicians are willing to ask. Many physicians still are unwilling to ask market-level fees, or are uninformed about what the market will allow. Fee schedules are easy to adjust, but just as easily overlooked.

Payer Mix

The group's financial well-being is strongly influenced by the diversity of insurance plans in its market, and the diversity of plans in which it chooses to participate. If the market is dominated by low-paying government programs or highly competitive managed care plans, the group may have little to say about how financially fit they will be. The payer mix is a product of the local economy, the demographics of the market and the presence or absence of market-savvy insurers. Changing the payer mix is a difficult process, and it assumes that competitors will be willing and able to care for patients that a group practice chooses not to focus on. If there are no alternatives for those patients, they'll end up back in the waiting room of the practice that didn't want them. In smaller communities where competition is limited, the payer mix is inherent with the region. If a physician wants a different payer mix, she may have to move to a different community.

Strategies for changing the payer mix may be beyond the scope of this book, but designing compensation systems requires at least a fundamental knowledge of change tactics, if compensation is to be understood in the context of the payer mix. The tactics may take years to have an impact, but they include strategies such as closing the practice to patients with undesirable insurance coverage, limiting the number of appointment slots for those patients, or simply de-participating with selected plans. Of course, those lost opportunities will have to be replaced by more lucrative uses of time and better-paying patients. Adjusting the payer mix is likely to have ramifications for longstanding patient relationships, practicalities for administering the new policies, and potential for negative public relations. That's why it may be the most difficult to change, and among the least favorite issues to tackle in compensation planning.

Coding

The group's financial success is affected by hundreds of decisions made each day by each physician about what the patients' needs are, what interventions are called for, who will provide those interventions, and ultimately, what current procedural terminology (CPT) code best describes the services provided. Coding patterns can vary widely in medical practices. Some physicians are better at documenting than others, and therefore can support more aggressive codes than their conservative (or rushed) colleagues.

Coding is an art and science of its own. Astute billing staff can monitor reimbursement patterns, payer by payer, and refine their coding processes over time. Wise managers are also willing to invest in regular seminars and publications to keep the billing staff up to date with the rapid changes in the field. In many offices, coding is a joint responsibility of both physicians and support staff, requiring a high level of communication and feedback about the results of coding decisions.

Competition

Physicians in communities that have more physicians in the same specialty than can be supported will face the cruel reality of the laws of supply and demand at some point. Health care is less responsive to the traditional economic forces found in other industries, but a glut of physicians in any specialty will make for tighter belts than might be found where the specialty is in shortage. Macroeconomic forces may cause individual physicians to feel that they are not getting their fair share, when the reality may be that there are more physicians in the community than there were formerly.

Intensity

Intensity is a measure of the degree of technical difficulty and risk that physicians are willing to bear in patient care. Physicians usually determine which specific procedures and services they will provide based on their training, their interests, and the needs of the group within which they practice. The intensity of their practice reflects these choices, and can be quantified through an analysis of the relative value units (RVUs) per encounter of each physician. Those who are procedure-intensive will generate higher RVUs per encounter than those who are more "cognitive" physicians.

Time Efficiency

The factors that physicians have most direct control over are how long, how diligently, and how efficiently they are willing to work. In a fee-for-service environment, hard work, long hours, and intense services can be rewarding financially when all the other factors are working as well. Physicians' time management counts for a great deal, especially when there is a greater demand for care than there is a supply of physician time, as is most often the case. Volume and intensity work hand-in-hand to optimize revenue under fee-for-service, and time management brings all the factors together.

Collections

The practice that tries hard to capture the greatest reimbursement for its medical services has a distinct advantage over the practice that ignores collections. The greater the discipline used in screening and registering patients, collecting payment at the time of service, timely billing, and consistent follow-up, the greater the collection ratios. Practices with strong collection ratios simply make the best cash flow of the work their physicians have already performed.

Overhead

Managing nonphysician expenses wisely results in more distributable revenue for the physician-owners in any market. In a group setting, this is frequently a role granted to a medical group administrator with oversight by the physicians, but the complex dynamics at work in every organization don't allow anyone the luxury of believing this important role can be completely delegated. A highly productive group that fails to watch its expenses can fare about as well as a low-productivity group that exercises discipline in purchasing and staffing.

The Medical Group Management Association (MGMA) conducted an information exchange questionnaire in 1998 inquiring about distribution formulas. They specifically focused on what expenses are charged back to physicians before calculating bonuses. They also asked how the charge-back system affected productivity or overhead. The comments showed a fairly consistent pattern. Physicians who are personally responsible for managing certain expenses pay closer attention to controlling overhead costs than those who don't face charge-backs.

In 2001, when the association conducted another questionnaire on physician compensation, they asked different questions, but the report demonstrates a remarkable quality about compensation plans. Of about 500 responses, over 100 described their formula as not fitting any typical type category such as equal share, straight salary, salary plus bonus, or production. One fifth of the respondents were sure that their formula was unique, and could only be classified as "other."

MGMA is also an excellent resource for research on overhead structures in medical group practices. The annual *Cost Surveys* detail the results of thousands of groups in all the major specialties, showing overhead costs in dollars and as a percent of net revenue, with breakdowns by expense categories.

Compensation Systems

Physician compensation is based upon the internal agreements physicians make with each other. This may be the topic of greatest discussion in groups, especially when several members are dissatisfied with their incomes. It is important to understand, however, that a compensation system cannot solve problems created by poor markets, too much competition, undisciplined management or collections, or extensive physician time-off. Compensation systems only help in deciding how to split the pie. The size of the pie is determined by these other factors.

The physicians who seem most interested in reviewing their compensation formula are those who are experiencing some sort of overall dissatisfaction with their incomes. The compensation formula seems like an easy target for that dissatisfaction, but it may be the wrong target. The practices that have a strong market position and strong management are more likely to be satisfied with their compensation system, regardless of what system they apply. Wise distribution systems are simply no substitute for wise management and marketing.

Quality as a Productivity Measurement

There are few practitioners who would disagree that quality of care is important enough to make a part of physician compensation, but there is plenty of disagreement about how to measure it fairly. Early attempts at measuring quality have focused on peer reviews, patient satisfaction surveys, and compliance with external requirements such as those held by HMOs. A few groups tie a small portion of their at-risk compensation to those measures. More advanced groups have begun to look at outcomes measurements to determine the most cost-effective ways of treating particular disorders. Overall, our collective wisdom about how to measure quality is rudimentary—perhaps at a level 2 or 3 on a scale of 10. Information systems need refinement beyond the capacity most small groups can currently afford, and the science of outcomes measurement has yet to deliver results that the average physician can rely upon to improve the quality of care. Those who are at the leading edge of outcomes measurement are likely to have a distinct advantage over their peers as markets become more competitive and groups seek to distinguish themselves. Even rudimentary measurements of quality can be useful if they become a part of the reward system.[10]

PREDICTION PROBLEMS

Understanding the factors of production under fee-for-service is important, but not sufficient to obtain desired compensation results. Physicians and their managers still need to manage each component to the extent they can be managed, if they want to maximize profitability. In reality, each factor is a moving target, changing to some degree by the impact of changes in the other factors. For example, adjusting fees will affect collection ratios, merging with competitors may affect the payer mix and the fee schedule, and investing in better collections systems will affect overhead. Nothing stays the same, and prediction becomes little more than an educated guessing game. That does not mean the group should avoid modeling its compensation plan; it simply means that the model should be understood and used with the flexibility inherent in its assumptions about the factors of production.

Spreadsheets can be wonderful tools in predicting the impact of changes in each of these assumptions. They can produce mouth-watering prospects with penny-perfect accuracy. The risk, however, is that physicians' expectations can be based on wishful thinking rather than market realities. Under those circumstances, even a well designed compensation formula can become the target of angst for disappointed physicians.

Some administrators have found that the best alternative is to model compensation plans with a range of assumptions. They may show a best-case scenario, tempered by a worst-case scenario. By using the rounding function in Excel to round results to the nearest $10,000 (and maybe even to round down), physicians are less likely to be fooled by the exquisite precision of income predictions based on wildly chaotic assumptions. Keeping them informed about how the key factors of production are actually turning out, month by month, is the key to minimizing the risk of unwelcome surprises.

THE MYTH OF EWYK

This chapter would not be complete without some discussion about a prevailing myth in physician compensation plans, particularly found where fee-for-service dominates the payer mix. The myth is that compensation can be based on production in a straightforward fashion. It has often been labeled with the repulsive and contra-Hippocratic name of "Eat What You Kill."

By now it should be clear that production is never straightforward, even in environments where fee-for-service is the dominant form of reimbursement. The production of every physician is a team effort. It is the result of physicians working with physicians, supported by skilled and loyal staff, representing the qualities that attract and retain patients of various economic conditions, medical needs, and relationships. Blatant claims to the personal production of any physician are an insult to everyone else in the practice. They ignore the realities of organizations and markets, and disrespect the contributions of hard-working staff. Highly productive physicians ought to earn above-average compensation. No one can begrudge that. But every physician should understand that productivity is the result of interdependent relationships among people and forces that are beyond his or her individual control.

I recommend that we slay the myth of EWYK, once and for all.

CASE EXAMPLES

Example A

A seven-physician primary care group grew discontented with its below-market compensation, and launched a comprehensive review of its factors of production. With 90 percent of its revenues based on fees for service, the group compared its own performance to benchmarks of visit volume, clinical time in the office, collection ratios, coding patterns and fee schedules. They quickly recognized a combination of group factors and individual factors that compromised their performance.

They initiated a variety of efforts, both as a group and as individuals. As a group, they re-examined their fee schedule and made changes to bring it consistent with the market. They also scrutinized their collections processes and developed tighter policies for permitting write-offs. They committed to update their coding knowledge as a group, and began to have regular discussions about individual cases, to improve coding consistency.

Individual physicians went beyond the group's initiatives by carefully re-examining their personal priorities, adjusting beginning and ending times for patient appointments, and considering their interests in developing new procedural skills. One of the family physicians decided to discontinue providing obstetrical services, and two others committed to updating their colonoscopy skills. A year later, physician profits were up about 20 percent from the prior year.

Example B

A 24-physician multispecialty group used a compensation system based on baseline salaries associated with thresholds of individual charges, varied by specialty, plus an incentive of a fixed percent of net charges in excess of the baseline threshold. The group found that some physicians were satisfied to perform at minimally acceptable levels, even as reimbursement rates were declining, compromising the ability of the organization to fully fund its retirement plan.

Their discontent led to a re-negotiated compensation plan that was based on receipts rather than charges. The new formula also adjusted the base salaries to require higher net receipt thresholds, making the minimal performers deliberately uncomfortable. All but one physician began to pay closer attention to their actual receipts, and found the motivation to increase volume and intensity of services to attain the higher thresholds. The one remaining low performing physician decided it was time to retire.

Models

What follows are several models that demonstrate how compensation can reward productivity under fee-for-service. Each model measures and rewards the most productive physicians, but in different ways. The examples pertain to typical primary care practitioners, but can be modified for any specialty by using market-specific data on charges and base compensation.

Model A

The first alternative is to consider a system that offers a negotiated base salary, plus a percent of gross charges over a certain threshold, to a market-reflective ratio of compensation-to-charges. Let's say that the target, based on MGMA data, tells us that the median ratio of compensation to charges for primary care physicians should be 0.44. Therefore, examples might be as follows:

	Degree of Risk		
	Low	**Medium**	**High**
Charges	$330,000	$330,000	$330,000
Base salary	$120,000	$100,000	$80,000
Plus bonus based on	40%	50%	60%
Of charges in excess of	$270,000	$240,000	$220,000
Would yield a bonus of	$24,000	$45,000	$66,000
For a total compensation of	$144,000	$145,000	$146,000
For a compensation to charges ratio of	0.44	0.44	0.44

The base salary, bonus percentage and threshold can all be negotiated between the physician and the employer, so long as the resulting target compensation is no more than the market ratio of compensation to charges. The initial target of charges for a mature practice would most likely be the previous year's charges.

Physicians who elect lower salaries and greater performance incentives stand to gain greater total compensation than those who elect higher salaries. The following example demonstrates what happens to total compensation when the provider in the previous example performs with charges at $360,000 instead of $330,000.

	Degree of Risk		
	Low	**Medium**	**High**
Charges	$360,000	$360,000	$360,000
Base salary	$120,000	$100,000	$80,000
Plus bonus based on	40%	50%	60%
Of charges in excess of	$270,000	$240,000	$220,000
Would yield a bonus of	$36,000	$60,000	$84,000
For a total compensation of	$156,000	$160,000	$164,000
For a compensation to charges ratio of	0.43	0.44	0.46

In this example, a 10 percent increase in production under the higher-risk option would yield $8,000 more in total compensation than the same increase in production under the low-risk option ($164,000 compared with $156,000). The incentive to increase production rewards both the individual physician and the employer.

The potential for strong rewards for top performers may lead to excessive production at the risk of declining quality of care. Model A contains no limits to what physicians can achieve financially. If the model is implemented, the organization will have to monitor other factors of physician performance to assure that quality of care is preserved and developed.

Startup practices would require targets of compensation-to-gross ratios to be multiples of those found in mature practices. In a typical market, a new practitioner can expect the practice to reach maturity by the third year. Therefore, the target for Year One might be 300 percent of the compensation-to-gross ratio (or 1.32 in the case of primary care), 200 percent in Year Two and 100 percent in Year Three. If the practice grows more rapidly than the targets, an additional fixed-amount bonus might be offered at year's end.

If a physician fails to produce according to his/her targets, the physician and the management team may need to re-evaluate the factors of production, or adjust the schedule, promotional efforts, or scope of services to better serve the target population. Two consecutive years of under-performance should be cause for discussions about whether the relationship is a good fit. Some practices may be worth sustaining continuing losses because of their strategic position or value to the organization's overall purpose, but the organization must be careful not to extend its developmental resources to the point that the long-term financial viability of the community institution is at risk.

It is critical to structure the compensation agreements a year in advance. Both sides must live with some degree of risk, for the relationship to be balanced. Each party must be committed to the success of the agreement by understanding what is expected up front, and supporting each other in achieving the incentives outlined in the agreement.

Finally, we recommend that bonuses be calculated and distributed quarterly. If physicians elect lower base salaries, they should not be required to wait until year's end to receive a substantial bonus. A quarterly distribution should serve well as a regular reminder of performance well done. If a bonus is not earned in a particular quarter, the physician should not be required to repay any portion of previously earned bonuses or to forgo a portion of his/her secure salary base.

The features and benefits of model A are:

- Physicians are rewarded for their production, the number one performance factor in their priorities, according to our research.

- Physicians can choose the degree of risk/security they desire. If they choose a higher base salary to reduce their risk, their potential total compensation will be less than if they opt for a lower salary and higher percent of bonus or lower threshold.

- Market-relevant ratios of compensation-to-gross charges are readily available from MGMA for all specialties, including nonphysicians providers, and they have shown little variance over time.

- Managing the collection processes and overhead costs well will reward management. If charges are collected at national-average levels or above, the institution may realize a benefit. Also, if the ratio of nonphysician costs-to-charges is maintained at or below market levels, the practices can be profitable.

Model B

Under the second model, current agreements for base salaries could be honored for the initial year, but the bonuses would be based upon a blend of production criteria and cooperation with management in effecting strategic changes necessary for long-term development. The base salaries may require adjustment in subsequent years based upon performance and market trends.

The two critical features of Model B are the creation of a *bonus pool* for each sub-practice in a group that has multiple specialties or multiple sites, and a *method* of distributing the bonus.

The bonus pool could simply be determined to be a percentage of net receipts for the sub-practice. The initial recommendation is that the pool be 6 percent of net receipts, which is roughly 15 to 20 percent of projected physician compensation for family practice. Focusing on net receipts rather than gross charges calls attention to the physicians' role in marketing to a representative payer mix, and cooperating with management and the support staff in properly coding and collecting for services performed. By using the net receipts for the sub-practice, the incentive system would call attention to the value of cooperating with colleagues to develop the practice and increase its attractiveness to patients.

The bonus pool would then be segregated into two parts. The first part, equaling 80 percent of the bonus pool, would be distributed on the basis of the percent each physician contributed to the total charges for the sub-practice. The second part, equaling 20 percent of the bonus pool, would be distributed on the basis of a compensation committee's assessment of each physician's cooperation with change initiatives, cost reductions for the sub-practice, and leadership contributions for the practice.

An example of Model B is as follows:

	Doctor A	Doctor B	Doctor C	Total
Charges	$280,000	$350,000	$240,000	$870,000
Percent of charges	32%	40%	28%	100%
Net receipts	$250,000	$300,000	$200,000	$750,000
Bonus pool (6% of net receipts)				$45,000
Production segment (80% of bonus pool)				$36,000
Production bonus (applied as % of charges)	$11,520	$14,400	$10,080	
Committee assessment bonus (20% of bonus pool)				$9,000
Assessment scores	10.2	14.5	6.3	31.0
Percent of assessment scores	33%	47%	20%	100%
Assessment bonus (applied as % of scores)	$2,970	$4,230	$1,800	
Total bonus above base salaries	$14,490	$18,630	$11,880	$45,000

The compensation committee would consist of two members of the management team and one physician. Each of the three members of the compensation committee would prepare their assessment of each physician based upon a simple analysis using the format shown below. The scores would be totaled to yield a single measurement for each physician.

Evaluate your appreciation of the physician's performance with respect to:

	Low				High
1. Cooperation with change initiatives	1	2	3	4	5
2. Cost reduction efforts	1	2	3	4	5
3. Leadership contributions	1	2	3	4	5

The scores would be averaged among the evaluators for each physician, and subtotaled for the sub-practice. The committee portion of the bonus would be based upon the percent of the sub-practice total each physician achieved. As the group functions more as a single group in a central location, the bonus pool might be applied to the entire group rather than to the sub-practices.

Base salaries for physicians in startup situations would be based on the national and local market dynamics, with the understanding that the model would apply when the practice has reached maturity, typically by about the third year of operation. Physicians joining a sub-practice would not participate in the bonus pool until their charges reach the 25th percentile according to MGMA data.

The features and benefits of Model B are:

- This model provides the least disruption to current base salaries in the first year, although modifications to base salaries may be necessary in incremental steps in subsequent years, to enable total compensation to reflect the market.

- Physicians will benefit from cooperating with management's initiatives to prepare for managed care, reduce overhead, and develop leadership skills.

- Individual production still plays a prominent role in determining individual compensation, but it is balanced by other critical dynamics that impact the organization's overall success.

- The model encourages physicians to develop each other in the sub-practice setting, since the bonus is based in part on their collective performance.

- The model can be modified over time to place greater emphasis on qualitative factors, as fee-for-service diminishes and managed care plays a greater role in the community.

Model C

The third alternative compensation model blends physician incentives found under a fee-for-service system with those found under capitation. It is designed to function as a transitional model as managed care penetration rises from zero to about 30 to 40 percent of the market share. Under capitation, physicians will be paid a monthly fee per patient, plus a portion of the savings they achieve by managing patient referrals to specialists, ancillary services and hospital care more efficiently than they would under fee-for-service incentives. The most profitable physicians in a managed care environment are those who manage a high volume of patients with preventive and appropriate services that result in increasing the health of the population while diminishing total health care costs.

The model works like this:

Factor	Calculation
Production	30% of net receipts on fee-for-service charges + 100% of capitation payments + 50% of risk payments and withhold payments received
Patient satisfaction	Overall % of satisfaction x $10,000
Peer review	Overall % of satisfaction x $10,000
Cost containment	Up to $10,000 based on a pre-determined index

The model can be adjusted to reflect the degree of managed care penetration, starting out with greater emphasis on the production and rotating toward a greater emphasis on quality and outcomes measurements as they evolve.

Measuring production under this model is likely to be quite straightforward. The three other factors in this model will require the development of tools that can be applied consistently and effectively. Generic resources are readily available to monitor patient satisfaction in office-based practices.

Peer review models are less standardized in the industry at this point. A simple method would be to develop a questionnaire for each physician to prepare in reference to every other physician in the practice. The questions might be comparable to those found in the peer review sample below.

Cost containment bonuses might be tied to performance relative to budgeted overhead expenses, or they might be indexed to MGMA median expense ratios. An example of an indexed system might be as follows:

Actual overhead per physician	MGMA median	Ratio	Bonus
$240,000	$200,000	120%	$0
$200,000	$200,000	100%	$5,000
$160,000	$200,000	80%	$10,000

Peer Review Questionnaire

Physician being reviewed:

Date of review:

	Least					Most

1. How has the physician's role in leadership contributed to the organization's advances this year? 0 1 2 3 4 5

2. How has the physician benefited the group with ideas and initiatives? 0 1 2 3 4 5

3. To what extent has the physician's contribution to discussion been helpful in advancing the group's interests? 0 1 2 3 4 5

4. How well does the physician appear to be an ambassador for the group within the hospital and the community? 0 1 2 3 4 5

5. How effective does the physician appear to be in satisfying patients' expectations for quality care? 0 1 2 3 4 5

6. How effective is the physician in making medical decisions? 0 1 2 3 4 5

7. How efficient does the physician seem to be in achieving positive medical results with limited resources? 0 1 2 3 4 5

8. How helpful are the physician's medical records habits for providing continuity of care? 0 1 2 3 4 5

The features and benefits of Model C are:

- The model can reward physicians under both fee-for-service and managed care incentive systems without conflict.

- The model can be easily adjusted to place greater value on the factors for success under managed care as the market share of capitated patients increases.

- This model introduces quality of care as a factor for rewarding physicians, which physicians identify as a high priority for their motivation, and which they identified as something they can control. Rewarding physicians for their quality of care can be profoundly satisfying.

Other Models

Following are four other models that demonstrate simple fee-for-service compensation calculations. They are offered not as complete models, but rather as components that demonstrate alternative uses of the factors of production, and hint at the benefits of simplicity.

Simplified FFS Model

	Dr. A	Dr. B	Dr. C
Base salary	$80,000	$100,000	$120,000
FFS receipts	$240,000	$300,000	$430,000
Contribution to group	$160,000	$200,000	$310,000
Bonus eligible?	no	no	yes

Base salaries set at $200,000 contribution-to-overhead target, or 30% of last year's receipts, whichever is less.

Split year-end cash as % of contribution among stockholders who contribute > $200,000 to group.

Bonus Based on Visits

	Dr. A	Dr. B	Dr. C	Total
Base salary	$80,000	$80,000	$80,000	
FFS receipts	$225,000	$300,000	$400,000	
Contribution to group	$145,000	$220,000	$320,000	
Office visits	4,500	6,000	8,000	18,500
Bonus share (% of visits)	24.32%	32.43%	43.24%	

Equal base salaries, split year-end cash as % of visits among stockholders.

Bonus Based on Contribution to Overhead

				Total
Base salary	$50,000	$75,000	$100,000	
Fee-for-service receipts	$240,000	$300,000	$400,000	
Contribution to group (salary – receipts)	$190,000	$225,000	$300,000	
Baseline contribution	$200,000	$200,000	$200,000	
Excess	($10,000)	$25,000	$100,000	$115,000.
Bonus share (adj. % of excess cont.)	0.00%	20.00%	80.00%	

Set base salaries at 75% of last year's total compensation.

Split year-end cash as % of contribution to the group among stockholders.

Forgive negative excesses as long as contribution is at least 90% of baseline.

Additional discretionary stipends can be granted to office-holders if corporate goals are met.

Indexed Compensation Model in FFS Market

Base Salary	Plus incentive of: X %	Over	Taxes & Benefits of	Net Receipts of	Will net Comp. To Doctor	Contribution to Overhead
$100,000	30%	$180,000	$20,000	$300,000	$136,000	$144,000
$125,000	30%	$195,000	$20,000	$300,000	$156,500	$123,500
$150,000	30%	$210,000	$20,000	$300,000	$177,000	$103,000
$100,000	30%	$180,000	$20,000	$400,000	$166,000	$214,000
$125,000	30%	$195,000	$20,000	$400,000	$186,500	$193,500
$150,000	30%	$210,000	$20,000	$400,000	$207,000	$173,000
$100,000	40%	$180,000	$20,000	$500,000	$228,000	$252,000
$125,000	40%	$195,000	$20,000	$500,000	$247,000	$233,000
$150,000	40%	$210,000	$20,000	$500,000	$266,000	$214,000

CONCLUSION

Fee-for-service is not likely to fade from the medical group practice landscape forever. The familiar measurements may require modification or amendments, but physicians are likely to still depend on a curious mixture of market forces they can't control and personal efforts they can control. At the heart of fee-for-service models is the need to somehow keep the rewards consistent with workloads. Nobody wants to be taken advantage of, and everybody wants their reward to be commensurate, in some way, to their efforts. Mutual trust is critical in group practices, but that trust must also be verified, even if the measurements are imprecise.

Even as managed care jockeys for position in the industry, the dynamics of working hard and working smart will continue to play valuable roles. The familiar measurements may require modification or adjustment, but physicians are likely to still depend on a curious mixture of market forces they *cannot* predict and personal efforts they *can* control.

The good news is that physicians can choose their own strategies in boosting production. Some strategies require the consensus of the whole organization, but others can be deployed individually, and are clearly within the control of the individual physician. To some degree, each physician can choose his/her own method for increasing productivity, based on interests, personal priorities, and market needs. The power of personal choice with these factors can give physicians the freedom to set their own goals for compensation within the boundaries of the market and the group's internal agreements.

5

Managed Care Compensation Models

DEBORAH L. WALKER, MBA, FACMPE

INTRODUCTION

There has been an increasing trend toward productivity-based physician compensation plans, with 40 percent of established primary care physicians and 34 percent of established specialists reporting compensation plans that involve an exclusive focus on individual productivity measures.[11] The benefits of these plans relate to the expectation that production-based formulas will encourage physicians to develop and maintain high productivity levels, whether measured by gross charges, net revenue, work relative value units, panel size, patient visits or some other related index.

More recently, however, a number of health care leaders who have been strong proponents of production-focused compensation plans have questioned whether these types of plans continue to be aligned with the goals and objectives of the medical group or of the integrated delivery system in which a medical group resides. Specific drawbacks of rewarding clinical productivity based on individual physician performance include:

- An exclusive focus on individual production at the expense of developing a group practice approach to patient care delivery;

- A reduced focus on cost of practice and overhead expenditures levels;

- A disconnect between clinical production and other important goals and objectives of the medical group, such as patient access and service; and

- The inability to exercise successful leverage and intervention with physicians who elect to perform at low production levels and who are not motivated by the financial incentive inherent in production-driven compensation plans.

These drawbacks have led health care executives to explore a transition from an exclusive focus on individual productivity to include group-level incentives and efficiency-based performance indicators. Many medical practices have now evolved to a hybrid compensation plan that includes production-based measures along with efficiency-based measures to permit alignment of the compensation plan with the goals and objectives of the medical practice and the overall integrated delivery system (as applicable). This hybrid approach toward performance measures and rewards is not only consistent with the dynamics and complexities of the current health care environment, but also consistent with knowledge workers operating in a knowledge economy, where there is a high value placed on self-coordination and self-control.[12]

Most medical groups today have a significant "managed care" component. Managed care extends well beyond capitation contracts to encompass patients covered by insurance plans that require a new type of infrastructure to "manage" the patient's care, such as managing second opinions, providing prior authorizations, using drug formularies, and tracking the use of ancillary services. Due to the need to manage care proactively in an environment of declining reimbursement, physician compensation plans that solely focus on individual physician productivity are not aligned with other important dimensions such as cost, quality and service. Therefore, the ability of the practice to compete effectively for managed care contracts and to achieve a positive financial position may be compromised as the practice undertakes risk contracting (including deeply discounted fee-for-service arrangements).

THE CASE FOR ACTION

Whether it is managed care, managed health, managed competition, or managed costs, the operative word is "managed." The goal for many medical groups is to "manage" the health experience of large panels of patients in order to meet the health care needs of their communities. This goal requires enhanced clinical productivity, resource optimization, utilization management, patient access and service, and demonstration of clinical outcomes within an efficient practice model. Consistent and active alignment of these elements by using management coordination systems, including the group's compensation plan methodology, is critical to ensure success.

Production-based compensation plans have been generally geared toward individual physician production. Combination plans or hybrid plans are emerging to recognize the need for alignment of the compensation plan with managed care and related practice goals. Many medical groups have elected to transition their compensation strategies to align them effectively with cost, quality, and service dimensions, rather than maintain an exclusive focus on production or productivity drivers. The measures that were historically viewed as critical for success in a fee-for-service environment are being supplanted with measures that permit alignment of the medical group toward its strategic and operational goals within the current dynamic and complex health care environment. Table 1 outlines the important differences in traditional fee-for-service and current managed care environments.

Many medical groups are also shifting their emphasis from a reliance on individual physician performance to one that recognizes the importance of group practice performance. Recognizing the need to develop patient care delivery models and staffing support models that take advantage of economies of scale and scope, many medical practices are developing compensation plans that focus on productivity of the group as a whole, rather than exclusively at the individual physician level. This approach to physician compensation

Table 1   The Case for Action

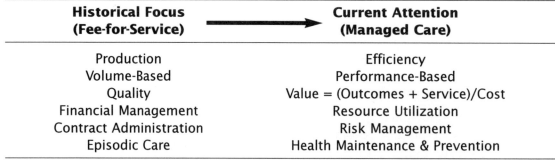

Historical Focus (Fee-for-Service)	**Current Attention (Managed Care)**
Production	Efficiency
Volume-Based	Performance-Based
Quality	Value = (Outcomes + Service)/Cost
Financial Management	Resource Utilization
Contract Administration	Risk Management
Episodic Care	Health Maintenance & Prevention

emphasizes the development of a true group practice mentality and culture, rather than simply co-locating individual practices within a single physical facility and providing shared call arrangements.

The attention to practice profitability is particularly heightened in today's health care environment. According to the MGMA 2001 Cost Survey, hospital-owned multispecialty practices are losing a median of $73,000 per FTE physician. These levels of financial loss will be difficult to sustain for any integrated delivery system. As a consequence, physician practice models are being scrutinized to ensure efficiency, productivity and profitability involving a review of physician productivity, support staff levels, support staff skill mix, the number of patients seen per scheduled clinic hour, patient scheduling systems, telephone management systems and other related factors. These systems are being reviewed to determine whether the cost of practice within a particular site or incurred by a particular medical group is appropriately aligned with physician work levels.

The disadvantages of utilizing the historic fee-for-service-designed compensation plans in the current health care environment are outlined in Table 2. The impact to the organization of a misaligned compensation strategy is great, often leading to poor financial performance and lack of attention to critical dimensions of patient access, service, and profitability.

Table 2 What Are the Disadvantages?

Typical Fee-for-Service Performance Measures	Disadvantages in Current Health Care Environment
Charges per Physician	Failure to understand contractual adjustments Lacks focus on resource utilization Lacks focus on patient satisfaction No group practice orientation
Collections per Physician	Differential income based on payer mix Lacks focus on resource utilization Lacks focus on patient satisfaction No group practice orientation
Patients Visits and/or Procedures	Encourages "churning" Lacks focus on resource utilization Lacks focus on patient satisfaction No group practice orientation
Equal Distribution of Revenue	Fails to provide equal pay for equal work No direct incentives to align behavior Lacks focus on resource utilization Lacks focus on patient satisfaction
Set Dollar for Hours/Week or Patients/Month	Minimum threshold may fail to motivate Lacks focus on resource utilization Lacks focus on patient satisfaction No group practice orientation

Mission, Vision and Values

The compensation plan architecture that is adopted by a medical group will depend upon the mission, vision, and values that have been embraced. Critical discussion of these dimensions is necessary in order to understand the basic underlying values of the group and to align compensation consistent with these values. Table 3 outlines questions to ask at this critical stage of incentive plan development.

Design Principles

Once the mission, vision and values are articulated, it is important for the medical group to articulate design principles of the compensation plan that are consistent with these elements. For example, if the group believes that meeting the health care needs of the uninsured or underinsured patient population is important, a compensation plan that relies solely on net revenue measured at the individual physician level would align behavior inappropriately. If the group believes that physicians should receive "equal pay for equal work," then a portion of compensation based on physician work levels could be included as alignment, along with a focus on other dimensions or perhaps on group-level production as well. As a final example, if a group believes that quality, cost-effective care is its mission, then compensation aligned with resource utilization and clinical outcomes would permit opportunity to align physician compensation consistent with these important values.

Design principles should be established prior to attempting to develop the plan architecture, so that the resultant plan can be compared with the design principles to ensure congruence. The design principles also assist in keeping the compensation development process on a consistent track related to overall medical group goals and objectives. Design principles for compensation plans typically include the following elements:

- Relatively few performance measures (typically less than 10);
- Well defined and understood goals and measures;

Table 3   What Are the Group's Values?

- Align compensation with work effort?
- Promote group culture?
- Reward "rainmakers"?
- Provide health care services to under-insured?
- Attract and retain quality physicians?
- Ensure cost effective, quality care?
- Enhance patient access and service?
- Meet financial targets?
- Improve service to referring physicians?
- Permit "balanced" life style for providers?
- Facilitate research?
- Educate medical students and residents?
- Others?

- Measures within the physician's control;
- A clear relationship between the measures and the desired behavior;
- Measures presenting a balanced set of performance expectations; and
- Measures relevant for "managing care" in the current health care environment.

Physicians who elect to practice in a medical group with their colleagues typically find that individual physician outlier behavior can no longer be tolerated due to the consequences of this behavior for the entire group. Poor performance on managed care report cards, physician profiles and patient satisfaction surveys may lead to contract termination (or non-renewal) or, at the very least, problematic re-negotiation of managed care contract terms. The compensation plan should not take the place of a physician performance management process. A well defined performance management process that has leverage to change physician outlier behavior is still necessary. The physician compensation plan can be aligned with expected performance, but it should not be relied upon exclusively to manage individual physician problematic performance.

COMPENSATION PLAN ARCHITECTURE

The overall compensation plan architecture can be selected from a number of frameworks, but some type of incentive plan is typically incorporated. A recent survey of practices conducted by the Medical Group Management Association (MGMA) reflects a shift from an exclusive focus on individual physician productivity to base-plus-incentive plans. Practices participating in the MGMA's 2001 Physician Compensation and Production Survey reflected the adoption of hybrid compensation models that involve various combinations of guaranteed base salary plus incentive (described as 50-99 percent productivity and 51-99 percent guaranteed salary arrangements). Thirty percent of established primary care physicians and 26 percent of established specialists report a compensation plan methodology that focused on 50 to 99 percent individual productivity, with 20 percent of established primary care physicians and 18 percent of established specialists reporting a plan that involves 51 percent to 99 percent guaranteed salary.

The actual compensation plan framework that is adopted by a medical group will depend upon the group's approach to compensation. Two models commonly employed are the base-plus-incentive plan and the XYZ plan.

Base-Plus-Incentive Plans

A base-plus-incentive plan provides the opportunity for physicians to receive a base level of compensation, supplemented by incentive payments based on performance indicators that typically include both productivity and efficiency-based indicators. There are two basic variations on this model. One approach is to target a total compensation level, with a portion of the total placed "at risk" to be earned by the physician. Another approach is to target a base compensation level, above which incentives permit additional earnings (to a legally defensible level).

The base salary is typically determined by market rates or as a percent of past compensation. Ideally, base salary should also be tied to minimum performance levels. This plan permits articulation of performance expectations for all physicians in the group, with the understanding that a reduction in base will be instituted for those members unable to perform at the minimum acceptable levels. Thus, a performance "floor" is established for organizational members.

The incentive portion of compensation consists of a number of performance measures to be achieved in order to earn maximum incentives. The incentive payment is typically paid quarterly to physicians, based on their ability to achieve specified targets and goals.

The "trip-wire" to achieve changes to physician behavior is 25 to 40 percent of compensation "at risk;" however, many practices start at lower levels, for example, 10 percent with graduation up to the 40 percent level. Depending upon the basis for the incentive, for example, group performance or individual performance, there are opportunities to increase the "at risk" portion more aggressively. For example, a compensation plan that places a total of 40 percent of compensation "at risk" could be constructed with half of the "at risk" compensation dependent upon profitability at the group level, and the other half at risk depending upon individual performance involving a combination of measures. Table 4 outlines the basic components in a base-plus-incentive-arrangement.

A variation on the base-plus-incentive plan is for a compensation committee to review the last 12 months of a physician's performance. Applying the base-plus-incentive formula, the annual compensation for the physician for the subsequent year is then determined. The advantages of this compensation plan variation include a more stable distribution of revenue to the physician, as well as the ability to assure a sustained level of performance over a 12 month period in order to receive the full incentive portion of compensation.

XYZ Plans

XYZ plans include three discrete components of compensation: X, Y, and Z. The "X" is the base portion of compensation, the "Y" is considered supplemental compensation, and the "Z" incentive compensation. Table 5 reflects the basic system architecture of this type of physician compensation model.

The X, or base, portion of compensation is similar to that contained in the base-plus-incentive model. That is, the base portion of compensation is tied to minimum acceptable performance standards for the group.

Table 4   Base-plus-incentive Plan

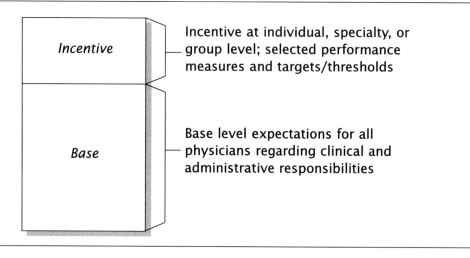

Table 5   XYZ Plan

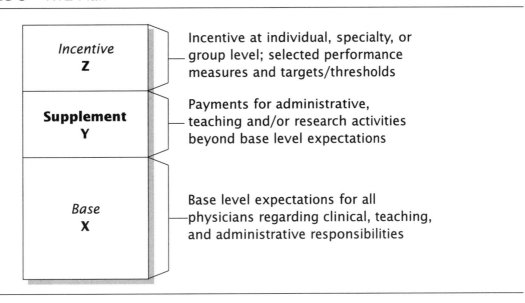

The Y, or supplement, is typically paid to physicians who have administrative roles within the group. This is often viewed as a stipend-like arrangement tied to specific duties such as medical directorship, committee chairs, and so on. The Y supplement can also be used to recognize portions of salary placed on research grants or other extramural funding sources.

The Z functions as the incentive portion of compensation, and fluctuates depending upon the physician's ability to achieve specific targets and goals. The incentive can include a combination of levels of incentive such as group-level measures, department-level-measures or individual-level measures, as well as both production and efficiency-based measures.

Performance Measures for Incentives

Categories for incentive performance measures include:

- Clinical productivity;
- Resource utilization;
- Patient satisfaction;
- Quality; and
- Leadership & citizenship.

A list of potential performance measures in each of these categories is provided in Table 6. In many instances, medical practices have elected to "roll up" a number of indices to one index of performance. For example, a patient satisfaction index involving results of patient surveys, member disenrollment, next available appointment, and patient waiting time in the reception area could be established. The physician is measured on performance involving each of these dimensions in order to receive the full portion of incentive devoted to patient satisfaction.

The selection of performance measures is one of the most critical elements in incentive plan development. The common phrase, "What gets measured gets done," is particularly

Table 6   Examples of Performance Measures

Clinical Productivity	*Performance Measures*	**Resource Utilization**
- Work Relative Value Units - Panel Size/Equivalents - Combination Measures		- Expenditures/RVU - Profitability - Ancillary Utilization
Patient Satisfaction	**Leadership & Citizenship**	**Quality**
- Report Card Scores - Waiting Times to Appointment - Disenrollment	- National Reputation - Contribution to Community - Teamwork & Collaboration	- Clinical Pathways - Outcomes Studies - Health Maintenance

true for physician compensation plans; thus, a careful and thoughtful approach toward performance measure selection, and financial modeling of the compensation plan based on historical data and future projections are key to developing an effective compensation plan.

Clinical Productivity

Physicians need to be highly productive in a health care environment of declining reimbursement, whether paid through a discounted fee-for-service arrangement or capitated on a per member per month basis. Many practices have pursued measures of clinical productivity that go beyond historical gross charges or net revenue approaches, to measures that are viewed as more "balanced" for a managed care environment and for a group practice approach toward patient care delivery. Three key measures of clinical productivity include the use of work relative value units (WRVU), panel size, and mixed measures such as a combination of panel size and patient visits.

Work Relative Value Units

The Work Relative Value Unit (WRVU) is one of three components of the Resource-Based Relative Value System (RBRVS) used by Medicare since January 1992 to reimburse for physician services. The RBRVS system essentially "maps" a relative value unit to a CPT code, attempting to approximate physician work levels, cost of care, and malpractice expense specific to the service provided. The WRVU permits examination of specific measures of physician work, including time spent before, during and after a service is performed, reflecting differences in physician work effort, resource costs and intensity across services.

In physician compensation plans, the WRVU is increasingly being adopted as a preferred measure of clinical productivity for a number of important reasons. First, WRVUs permit equity across specialties, enabling comparison of physician workload levels between, for example, surgeons and primary care physicians, thus focusing on equal pay for equal work. Secondly, unlike net collections, WRVUs evidence no discrimination for payor mix. Third, WRVUs also permit the practice to move beyond a gross charges/net collection mindset. This is particularly important for groups with a large number of managed care contracts, since reimbursement levels will typically vary considerably among contracts. It is also obviously important for those medical groups with capitation contracts where a gross charges/net collections mindset loses its relevance. Finally, there is an inherent value in using relative value units in analyzing the performance of the medical group, permitting the medical practice executive to analyze revenue and expense per RVU and per WRVU, compare expenditure levels with national norms, and/or develop a floor reimbursement or capitation rate.

Unfortunately, the disadvantages of utilizing only WRVUs to measure clinical productivity are similar to that of other clinical production measures. A focus on increasing WRVUs could conceivably result in increases to the volume of procedures or patient visits conducted. With a focus on WRVUs, some physician may begin to differentiate their clinical activity based upon WRVU production; for example, they could emphasize inpatient procedural activity at the expense of outpatient ambulatory practice. Thus, when WRVUs are utilized in physician compensation models, a heavy emphasis is placed on monitoring utilization and sharing this data with physicians and/or combining WRVUs with another index, such as unique patient visits, to serve to lessen the incentive to "grow" WRVUs.

Panel Size

Many practices in highly managed care environments use panel size in their approach to compensation. Some pay physicians a set dollar amount for panel size or panel size equivalencies. Other practices identify ranges of patient panel size and associated dollars per panel range. For practices that do not have contracts that relate to panel size, a proxy is typically used to determine the patient panel size for a physician. The unique patient visit count for the past 18 to 24 month period represents a generally accepted proxy for panel size for a physician. (Note, however, that when the unique patient count is calculated for the entire medical group, it is typically overstated, as patients may have seen more than one physician member of the medical group.)

Developing incentives around panel size or unique visits encourages market share growth. When unique visit counts or panel size is used in compensation methods, there is a reduced incentive to "churn" patients involving multiple return visits. This measurement of clinical productivity also tends to be consistent with "managing" the health care needs of the patient population and the introduction of outreach efforts for health maintenance and prevention.

The disadvantages of utilizing only unique visits or panel size to measure clinical productivity include the following:

- Lack of severity or risk adjustment of the panel;
- Lack of recognition of actual workload related to the panel, e.g., call schedules not equitable;
- Variation in panel size may be "random," e.g., a function of enrollment rather than reflective of discrete physician selection; and
- "Cherry-picking" with physicians attempting to select "healthier" patient populations.

Many practices are well beyond adjusting panels based only on gender and age. They have adopted case mix systems to effectively risk-adjust panels. A number of ambulatory case mix systems are currently in use, with many proprietary products on the market. A major difference among these systems is the focus used to explain the amount and type of resources utilized in the ambulatory visit. Some case mix systems focus on the visit itself and the services performed during the visit, while others focus on diagnoses and underlying health status of the patient. Failure to adjust compensation for the health status of patients reinforces risk selection by insurance carriers and providers. The advantage of using ambulatory case mix systems is their ability to equate workload levels within the practice, taking into account risk and severity adjustment of patient panels.

Mixed Clinical Production Measures

Mixed clinical production measures are often employed by medical practices. For example, a group level incentive may include a portion of net collections that are shared equally among physicians, combined with an individual level incentive based upon a combination of panel size and patient visits. These models can be highly complex or more simply defined; however, the combination of the levels of measures and the actual measures themselves need to be rationally defined and generally consistent with each other to ensure alignment.

Resource Utilization

As described earlier in this chapter, resource utilization and cost of patient care delivery are receiving heightened focus in today's health care environment. A number of performance measures that are used in this area are outlined in Table 6. One, in particular, that has received attention from a number of groups is related to revenue and expense per RVU and per WRVU. A ratio of revenue and expense per WRVU begins to equate physician workload with the revenues and expenditures associated with this level of clinical practice.

Another approach to measuring resource utilization is to apply the same or similar measures that are outlined in the group's managed care contracts in order to ensure consistency with contract terms to optimize revenue performance. Targets and goals for ancillary utilization, specialty referrals, pharmacy, and so on may be used to align physician behavior in accordance with contractual obligations of managed care contracts.

Patient Satisfaction

The impact of patient access and service dimensions continues to remain a leading factor for the selection of providers and integrated delivery systems by employers. Patient satisfaction survey instruments, while often criticized as being unreliable or invalid, continue to receive heightened attention, with the recognition that "perception is reality" within this dimension. Specific quantitative measures available to a medical practice include patient waiting time to appointment, and patient waiting time in the reception area. Many practices also identify a few critical questions from their patient satisfaction surveys and incorporate the results into the compensation plan performance measures. For example, three key questions could be identified as critical to the success of the medical group overall and could be used as a measure for patient satisfaction: (1) whether or not the patient would refer a family member or friend to the provider; (2) whether the patient's expectations were met; and (3) whether the patient's questions were answered satisfactorily. Other questions that the group has identified as relevant to measuring patient satisfaction could also be used.

It is important to recognize that beyond the primary customer—the patient—access and satisfaction measures can be obtained from employers, referring physicians and insurance carriers. Employing a number of measures of patient satisfaction and rolling these up to an index is often used to measure access and satisfaction levels involving patients and other important external constituents.

Quality

According to a number of health care futurists, measures of quality are expected to replace measures of service and cost and become the primary focus for health plan and patient selection of physicians and medical groups in the future. Most medical practices continue to struggle to determine the appropriate measures for demonstrating quality and clinical outcomes. For compensation purposes, many medical practices utilize compliance with clinical protocols and clinical pathways. Some measure Health Plan Employer Data and Information Set (HEDIS) indicators, others focus on assessment of health maintenance and prevention efforts, while still others focus on medical record documentation as measured by periodic chart reviews. A quality report card can contain multiple indices "rolled" into one to ensure an appropriate overall balance.

Leadership and Citizenship

The category of "Leadership and Citizenship" is often used to reward active involvement in professional societies, community leadership, and "rainmaking" type of behavior, for example, marketing the practice to the community and using one's own reputation to assist in increasing market share. This area of performance measurement is also often used to address group practice and team-oriented behaviors, and is the most subjective category of performance measures, with performance often assessed by the medical director rather than through discrete quantitative measures. Medical groups seeking to enhance their brand name in the market or community through recognition of physician leadership in professional and scientific efforts (which are often perceived by patients as an indication of "quality") use this performance measure to actively encourage high visibility leadership in the community.

Financial Structure for Incentives

A variety of financial approaches are used to determine income distribution for achievement of the targets or thresholds established for the incentive performance measures. These include:

- Set dollar values;
- Percentage of base compensation;
- Percentage of projected compensation; and
- Percentage of incentive pools.

Setting target levels for performance measures is not trivial, as particular approaches can provide disincentives for physicians or can foster behaviors that are unintended. External benchmark data are available for a number of measures including WRVUs and cost of practice overhead rates; however, it is important for physicians to embrace the benchmarks and believe in their validity. Many physicians believe that their patients are unique, either "sicker than" or "different from" patients seen in practices that contributed to the benchmark studies. However, when benchmarks are used to identify areas of opportunity, rather than as discrete targets and goals for performance, they can assist in identifying areas of performance that can be targeted for improvement.

The degree of improvement over a medical group's own internal baseline level is used as a specific target or goal by many practices. The advantages of using internal benchmarking data include moving the organization forward from its current state; however, disadvantages to this approach are many. The current level of performance may be well below acceptable levels. In addition, if future incentives are predicated on past performance, physicians may be reluctant to exceed current targets and goals, since they recognize they will be asked to "outdo" themselves the following year.

Goals and targets should be realistic. While stretch goals are suggested, they should be perceived by physicians as achievable in order to foster motivation toward goal achievement. If the work effort to achieve a goal appears greater than the benefit, then physicians will forgo the benefit. When clinical indices are involved it is important that data be viewed over a long horizon, again mindful of not affecting clinical care delivery negatively.

While the overall compensation plan architecture can remain static, the performance measures and targets will change over time. For example, as a resource utilization measure, the medical practice may target a reduction in expense per WRVU by 10 percent this year, with a focus on matching staffing levels and staffing skill mix to productivity levels the following year. As this example demonstrates, the overall compensation plan architecture remains intact. Resource utilization has been selected as a performance measure; however, the actual performance measures and targets vary each year, depending upon the medical practice's goals and objectives.

INCENTIVE PLAN DEVELOPMENT

The following areas are critical for incentive plan development.

Legal Counsel Review

It is important to involve legal counsel review of any incentive compensation plan that is constructed, in order to ensure that the compensation plan is consistent with Stark law, Anti-Kickback law, exempt status of the medical group, and other relevant laws and regulations.

Physician Leadership

Physician leadership in the compensation plan development process and in communication and implementation strategies is strongly recommended. Physicians who are affected by the plan must also be actively engaged in dialogue regarding the compensation plan, to ensure understanding and a high level of commitment to the goals and objectives of the plan. In many ways, the process of developing the compensation plan is just as important as the actual product. Physicians must have an active voice in compensation plan development, as its ultimate success will depend upon its perceived fairness and its alignment with the group's values.

Administrative Infrastructure

The administrative infrastructure required to identify and measure the performance indices must be addressed, including data capture, data accuracy, measurement and reporting, information technology and administrative support services. Physicians who have a significant portion of their compensation "at risk" must receive complete, accurate and timely reports regarding their performance, to permit opportunities for course corrections. Administration would be wise to audit their reports regularly for accuracy, since inaccuracy can undermine physician confidence.

CASE EXAMPLES

Three case examples are presented to provide examples of the above discussion. These examples are solely for the purpose of illustration. Readers are strongly encouraged to consult with legal counsel regarding compensation and incentive plan development to ensure compliance with relevant laws and regulations.

Case Example A

Case Example A is a 50-member multispecialty practice with primary care only. The physicians have historically been paid a negotiated salary, and they are transitioning to a base-plus-incentive compensation plan to include productivity and efficiency-based performance measures.

Base Component

Base Level of Compensation: Set at median market levels using a "blended" average of internal medicine, family practice and pediatrics benchmarks.

Expectations for Base Salary

Value	Performance Measure	Index	Level
Market Share Growth	Clinical Productivity	Median WRVU Levels On Call Expectations	Individual
Quality	Medical Record Documentation Clinical Guidelines	Chart Reviews Chart Audit	Individual
Service	Patient Satisfaction Survey	Minimum Acceptable Rating	Individual
Resource Utilization	Profitability	Budgeted Revenue/Expense	Group
Citizenship	Office and Committee Responsibility	Evidence of Active Contribution	Individual

Incentive Component

Incentive Level of Compensation: May earn an additional 20 percent of base as part of incentive portion of compensation.

Expectations for Incentive Payment

Value	Performance Measure	Index	Level	Weight
Market Share Growth	Clinical Productivity	Work RVU Net Collections	Individual Group	Total weight is 40%: Individual WRVU is 20% Group equal share based on net collections is 20%
Quality	Clinical Protocols	Development of New Protocols	Individual	10%
Service	Exemplary Service	Survey, Focus Groups	Group	20%
Resource Utilization	Cost of Patient Care Delivery	Expenditures Per WRVU	Group	20%
Leadership	Community Involvement	Demonstration of Extraordinary Efforts	Individual	10%

Case Example B

Case Example B is a 28-member multispecialty group practice. The medical group has historically been paid via 100 percent individual physician productivity based on net collections. It is transitioning to an XYZ model to develop a group practice approach to care delivery, to permit discrete compensation components, and to move beyond an individual physician production-focused mindset.

- **X (Base):** Similar to the previous model, a base set of expectations is determined based on benchmark levels. Each physician is expected to meet base-level performance, with compensation reduced in the event of non-performance.

- **Y (Supplement):** A supplement is paid to those physicians who perform administrative functions, for example, medical director, program coordinator, quality assurance committee chair and so on. For physicians who are actively involved in research, the portion of compensation paid via extramural funds is identified in the supplement component, with expectations for X (base) adjusted as appropriate.

- **Z (Incentive):** The group elects to "mimic" the requirements of the managed care plans for withholds and risk pools. Specifically, if the group is within acceptable target levels, physicians receive "bonus" or Z compensation in addition to X base plus Y supplement.

Case Example C

Case Example C is an 18-member single specialty group. The group has been functioning as a partnership with an equal share revenue distribution among physicians. The group desires to move beyond paying individuals the same rate, to reward physicians differentially for their work effort.

Base Component

Base Level of Compensation: Total compensation is set at 75th percentile of benchmark norms, with the base component set at median levels.

Expectations for Base Salary

Value	Performance Measure	Index	Level
Equal Pay for Equal Work	Clinical Productivity	Risk Adjusted Panel Size	Individual
Service	Patient Satisfaction Surveys	Target Levels for Satisfaction	Individual
	Next Available Appointment	Periodic Audits of Scheduling	Individual
Resource Utilization	Expenditures	Expenditures/visit	Group
Quality/Clinical Outcomes	Chart Documentation Health Maintenance & Prevention	Chart Audit Outreach Activities	Individual Individual
Esprit de Corps	Administrative Roles and Committees	Medical Director Assessment; Active Contribution and Involvement	Individual

Incentive Component

Incentive Level of Compensation: To receive the targeted total compensation, physicians must achieve incentive targets and goals. Performance measures are weighted, with weights totaling 25 percent.

Expectations for Incentive Payment

Value	Performance Measure	Index	Level	Weight
Equal Pay for Equal Work	Clinical Productivity	Encounters and WRVU, for Panel and Non-panel	Individual	20%
Quality	Clinical Protocols Readmissions	Development of New Protocols Readmission rates and Non-emergent ER Visits	Group	25%
Service	Referring Physician	Survey, Focus Groups	Individual	20%
Resource Utilization	Utilization Management	Visits, Ancillary Usage, Aggregate LOS	Group	25%
Leadership	Community Involvement	Demonstration of Extraordinary Efforts	Individual	10%

CONCLUSION

The importance of revisiting a medical group's physician compensation methodology, in order to move beyond a plan that solely rewards individual physician productivity, cannot be overemphasized. Continuing to adopt a productivity focus for physician compensation consistent with an individual practice and traditional fee-for-service mindset may have detrimental effects on the financial health of the medical group, and may compromise its ability to acquire and retain both patients and managed care contracts. Transitioning physicians (1) from an exclusive focus on productivity-based compensation to include efficiency-based indicators, and (2) from individual physician incentives to include performance measures at the medical group level, is highly consistent with the economics of the current health care environment. It will further assist physicians to align behavior consistent with group practice and with proactively "managing" the patient care delivery process.

6

A Checklist for Devising New Compensation Plans

KENNETH M. HEKMAN

The process of changing a compensation plan may be as important to its success as the design of the plan. In this chapter, we'll examine the steps involved and ask a few qualitative questions along the way to minimize the stress inherent in every change.

KNOWING WHEN TO CHANGE

If medical group administrators and physician leaders respond to every complaint about the compensation system as an indication that it's time for a change, they will never complete the process. The first critical step in making a change in the compensation system is knowing when a change is required. A pattern of consistent complaints from physicians may be an indicator that change is required, but it should not be taken at face value as the main reason for implementing a critique of the system. Complaints should be followed up with a series of studies benchmarking the compensation performance against national data such as the information from the annual MGMA physician compensation surveys. There may be about three general conditions under which the group may want to adjust its compensation system.

First, there may be a consistent pattern of complaints from physicians and/or from the staff. Physicians, of course, may have their issues on a continual basis. Staff, however, may make observations about how physician behavior is in conflict with smooth patient flow or collegiality within the group. If those behaviors are driven by compensation incentives inherent in the plan, it may be time for some reflection and refinement.

A second condition for change may come when there is a major adjustment in the group's strategy, payor mix or internal composition. If the group adds specialties or adopts a satellite strategy to increase its market share, the compensation system may require some adjustments to validate and fortify those strategies. If the group experiences a gradual change from fee-for-service to capitation, eventually the compensation system will require some adjustment to respond to the different incentives in each contract. Merging with another group, or other dramatic transitions in the composition of the group, are also likely opportunities to reexamine the compensation plan. At each of these junctures there are opportunities and challenges on which the compensation plan will have an impact. Its impact, however, should always be tempered with the impact of other policies and strategic changes that the management team might be able to make. Again, the compensation plan cannot solve every problem, but it should not be ignored in each major transitional situation.

The third reason to consider adjusting compensation is when the group is financially troubled. If profitability is lacking or overhead is raging out of control, the compensation system is likely to be one of several operational policies that can affect a turnaround.

WHO SHOULD BE AT THE TABLE?

Deciding who will be responsible for the ticklish decisions regarding compensation can be a sensitive indicator of what lies ahead. If every physician wants to be at the negotiating table, that is a pretty strong indication of the high emotions surrounding the compensation issue. If, however, the group is able to identify its representatives easily and entrusts them to represent the interests of the group as a whole, the outcome of the process is likely to be far more successful.

The question of who should be at the table has to be answered secondary to another question: Who trusts whom? The degree of representation is directly correlated to the level of trust among the physicians. The greater the distrust, the larger the compensation committee. If the leadership senses that everyone wants to be represented on the committee, it may be wise to defer the compensation discussions and focus first on trust-building within the group.

In a multispecialty setting, it is wise for each specialty, each service, and each clinical department to be represented in the compensation discussions. While the group may agree on its mission, vision and values, there are inherent qualities unique to each specialty that will require individual consideration. The overhead structure, the work flow expectations, and the size and make-up of each department will affect the uniqueness of each specialty. Some of those unique qualities may be discernible across specialties, but others will only be fully recognizable by those who are in each department. Engaging each department increases the opportunity for acceptance of the proposed compensation plan when it is ready for presentation.

The management team has a vital role in compensation planning. Their role will be to listen and discern the range of values expressed in the meetings, but also to model the suggested measurements for tracking physician behaviors. The administration will have a better handle than the physicians will have on what is practical for gathering data to support the compensation plan. Administrators can bring research to the discussions—research about benchmarks, about special situations and about tactics deployed in similar circumstances.

Compensation planning meetings should be relatively open affairs, once the assignment of trust has been granted and received. That is, there should be no secret meetings of individual members within the committee to politicize the outcome of the group's efforts. The trust that brought the representatives to the table must be preserved by remaining vulnerable and transparent in the discussions that will move the plan forward. If word of a back-office deal reaches the ranks of physicians who trusted their representatives to negotiate in good conscience, the potential for reaching an acceptable solution diminishes dramatically.

The challenge in constructing the compensation planning committee will be to affirm that all important segments of the organization are represented, while maintaining a task-oriented group that does not grow beyond its ability to make decisions. Size and representation are polarities to manage in the process of devising and designing a compensation plan.

DESIGNING A COMPENSATION SYSTEM

We will look at five specific components in the sequence of redesigning a compensation plan. You should understand, however, that while the steps may be predictive, the pace is not. The length of time required to compile the research, negotiate the terms of the new compensation plan, and implement it successfully can vary widely, from a few meetings to several months, depending on the complexity and level of trust within the group. Let's take a look, then, at the five steps in compensation planning, and explore evaluative questions to serve as a checklist or practical guide through the process of designing a compensation system.

FIVE STEPS IN THE PROCESS OF DESIGNING A COMPENSATION SYSTEM

1 Articulate what you want the compensation system to accomplish.

2 Look backward to compare how well the old system worked to accomplish the new goals.

3 Brainstorm how to better measure behaviors that support new goals.

4 Refine the model until you have agreement.

5 Evaluate the effectiveness of the new formula in the real world.

---

1. Articulate what you want the compensation system to accomplish.

A wise mentor once said, "A problem isn't a problem until you call it a problem." The wisdom is perhaps a derivative on the old saw, "If it ain't broke, don't fix it." Articulating what you want the compensation system to accomplish may not be as easy as it sounds. It is not as straightforward as it may appear, because the hidden message behind most physicians' concerns and complaints about a compensation system is that they wish their individual paycheck were greater. They may use terms like, "I wish the compensation system were more equitable," or "I wish the compensation system would reward productivity," but in effect, each discussion has to do with how the physician can lobby it to improve his or her own situation.

Articulating what you want the compensation system to accomplish might include making a list of the frustrations you have with the current system. It might also include making a list of the values that you feel are under-represented in the current formula. Some physicians might describe how they wish the formula would correct certain aberrant behaviors in their peers. The process at this stage is to identify the problems that require fixing or the refinements that can help the group accomplish its overall strategic goals. In other words, the first stage is articulating the issues that need to be rectified.

Following are some questions to ask in articulating what you want the compensation to accomplish:

1. How have changes in our corporate strategy impacted the behaviors we want to reward in the future?

2. How has our payor mix changed since the last time we adjusted our compensation system, and what impact might those changes have on future decisions?

3. Which benchmark comparisons, such as average physician compensation, overhead percentage, collection ratios, or panel sizes, identify potential problem areas in our compensation system?

4. How has the competitive marketplace changed, and how are those factors likely to affect our compensation system?

2. Look backward to compare how well the old system worked to accomplish the new goals.

Once you've articulated the ideals that you're hoping to accomplish, it may be valuable to measure how well the old system was working in accomplishing those goals. You may be surprised to find out, for example, that a group desiring to increase its productivity already has a system that perfectly correlates productivity with compensation using one particular measurement. Using the correlation coefficient function in Excel can be critical at this juncture.

This process of looking backward requires a qualitative analysis as well as a quantitative one. Even if certain measures were perfectly correlated, the group might not be getting the kinds of behaviors it wants to get, and that analysis can only come from honest reflection of the shortcomings and the dynamics of the former system. A few key questions to ask in Stage 2 are these:

1. What behaviors did the old system reward well?

2. What behaviors did the old system reward poorly?

3. How could the old system be manipulated for personal gain?

4. How well did physicians understand the impact their behavior had on their compensation?

5. Which issues did physicians actually have control over that could influence their compensation under the old system?

3. Brainstorm how to better measure behaviors that support new goals.

Compensation systems often get designed on the basis of convenient data rather than thoughtful ways to change physician behaviors. Once the group has identified the gaps between the ideals for the compensation system and the realities of the old system, it will have an opportunity to create fresh ideas about how to fill those gaps.

By definition, brainstorming is a process that requires people to set aside their personal feelings, to arrest their personal judgments for the benefit of the group. If committee members are honest with themselves and worthy of the trust they have been granted by their peers, they will use this step as an opportunity to think beyond their own individual agendas and to come up with ideas that reflect the values the group holds most dear. Creative committees will come up with ideas that may not be currently measured by any of the group's information systems. Compelling ideas, however, may spawn new ways of measuring physician performance. Drawing from the fields of clinical science and behavioral science, committee members may find that the best way to get what they want is to invent new tracking systems. Reinvention of tactics, however, should be reserved for those situations where none of the existing data systems can be modified to measure the desired behaviors.

Following are a few questions to stimulate the brainstorm:

1. If we were not constrained by the data we already know, how would we measure the behaviors for the most successful physicians in our group?

2. How could we measure and reward those physicians who provide the best patient care?

3. Which of our values should receive the highest rewards?

4. Which behaviors should be minimized, and how would we measure them?

4. *Refine the model until you have agreement.*

This step has several sub-parts to it. It assumes that the group answers the questions posed in the first three steps: articulating what the compensation system is to accomplish, identifying the gaps with the old system, and developing fresh ideas about how to measure the desired behaviors. The fourth step is perhaps the most artistic step. It requires assembling all of those value discussions and measurement experiments into a replicable formula that can be evaluated from several different perspectives.

Once alternative models have been explored, the group is likely to go through several iterations to refine its preferred method. The group would be wise to evaluate the best proposed methods against historical data to see what the compensation would have been if the new rules were applied in the recent past. It is also helpful to spell out what the minimum productivity requirements will be to accomplish physicians' compensation goals.

Excel spreadsheets are invaluable tools for modeling at this stage. They lend themselves to frequent modification and efficiently point the group toward outcomes it can live with. The modeling, however, is just one component of the refinement to take place in this stage of the process. The group also has to begin to share its findings with those who will be affected by the proposed compensation plans. Refinement comes through dialogue with those who will be affected, especially those on the upper and lower end of the spectrum of compensation. Refinement should be a time to reflect on the principles of the formula rather than to cut special deals, however, and refinement may take as long as it takes to build support for both the concepts and the consequences of the formula.

Following are some questions to ask during the refinement phase:

1. How would compensation have been affected if we used the new formula last year?

2. What impact would either growth or contraction of the group have on a compensation system?

3. How can we make the formula easier to administer?

4. How can we make sure we are monitoring the behaviors we will reward in a timely fashion?

5. How will we respond if a physician is not able to perform well under this new formula?

5. *Evaluate the effectiveness of the new formula in the real world.*

The work of the compensation committee is not done when the proposed formula has been accepted. The committee, or some derivative of the committee, should remain in place to monitor the effectiveness of the new formula for achieving the goals the group set out to accomplish. There should be periodic reviews of correlation coefficients between compensation and the measurements of physician behavior considered most valuable to the process. These reviews should occur annually after the final application of the compensation formula for the fiscal year.

The group may also want to establish an appeals process to contend with unintended consequences that arise from implementing the new system. If, for example, a previously productive physician becomes dispirited under the new formula, the appeals committee should listen to his or her concerns and reflect on them for insights about the design of the formula. If productivity goes up, but quality of care is compromised, the committee should maintain a system of identifying red flags that would require intervention.

The appeals committee does not have the job of satisfying every discontented physician under the new formula, but rather to clarify that the formula is achieving what it intended to achieve for the group as a whole. Consultants frequently remark that the indication of a good compensation system is one that leaves all physicians equally discontented. The appeals committee shouldn't necessarily expect to resolve those discontents, as much as to manage them.

Following are some questions to ask in the evaluation stage:

1. How well did the new formula accomplish the goals that we established in stage one?

2. What unintended consequences have arisen, and how can they be managed?

3. What market forces should we anticipate that might affect the effectiveness of the compensation system in the coming years?

4. How consistent is our compensation system with our mission, vision and values?

CONCLUSION

The process of change is rarely uncontroversial. Compensation committees will be called upon to exercise wise leadership in managing the diverse values, temperaments and nuances of each physician and each specialty within the group. Wise leaders will pay as much attention to the process as to the outcome, and realize that even the best ideas can be compromised by political blind-siding. Chapter 9 offers some additional insights to implementation from a physician's perspective.

7

Design Variances

KENNETH M. HEKMAN

We have seen the importance of a few founding principles in all physician compensation systems. We have looked at the principles of equity and fairness, of measuring revenues and costs, and of tailoring the compensation to the market dynamics as well as to the mission, vision and values of the group.

The application of those founding principles can vary significantly from one setting to another. In this chapter, we will examine some of the most prominent settings, and consider variances that might apply to the design and application of compensation systems based on the setting.

SINGLE SPECIALTY GROUPS

Single specialty groups are typically the most homogeneous model for developing compensation systems. The patterns of production may differ by the age and interests of the individual physicians, but the spread between the highest and lowest producers is usually much narrower than is found in multispecialty groups, and that seems to be an informal, but powerful indicator of fairness. When the highest producer is earning twice the amount of the lowest full-time producer in the same specialty, tension seems to mount. Such variances are far more tolerable in multispecialty groups, but single specialty groups need to pay attention to the spread with greater diligence, to maintain peaceful relationships among physicians.

The following example is a demonstration of how a single specialty group with a mixture of fee-for-service and capitation might handle physicians with a significant span of productivity.

Mixed Model Based on Contribution to Overhead

	Dr. A	Dr. B	Dr. C	Total
Base Salary	$50,000	$75,000	$100,000	
FFS Receipts	$160,000	$190,000	$240,000	
Capitation visits	1,000	1,400	1,800	4,200
Percent of cap. visits	23.81%	33.33%	42.86%	
Total HMO revenue				$300,000
HMO revenue applied as percent of visits	$71,429	$100,000	$128,571	
Total Revenue	$231,429	$290,000	$368,571	
Contribution to group	$181,429	$215,000	$268,571	
Baseline contribution	$200,000	$200,000	$200,000	
Excess	($18,571)	$15,000	$68,571	$65,000
Bonus Share (adj. percent of excess cont.)	0.0%	17.95%	82.05%	

Set base salaries at 75 percent of last year's total compensation.
Apply total HMO revenue (capitation and risk) as percent of HMO visits.
Add applied HMO revenue to net FFS revenue to determine contribution to group.
Split year-end cash as percent of contribution to the group among stockholders.
Forgive negative excesses as long as contribution is at least 90 percent of baseline.
Additional discretionary stipends can be granted to office-holders if corporate goals are met.

MULTISPECIALTY GROUPS

Multispecialty groups have dynamics that differ from single specialty medical practices in complex ways. There is often a deeper appreciation of the interdependence among specialties balanced by the tensions associated with concern about who is getting what slice of the production pie. Ultimately, each specialty department has to carry its own weight for the multispecialty practice to survive.

When designing compensation systems for multispecialty practices, it is important to look at the variances in overhead by each specialty. Surgeons, for example, will use considerably less office resources than primary care physicians. On the other hand, they may require more costly technical medical technology to perform office-based interventions.

The physician compensation system may become the battleground for some of the cultural challenges of a multispecialty group. It is not uncommon to see the compensation discussions give voice to jealousies or turf concerns among specialties. Primary care physicians who are procedure-intensive might feel that their territory is being infringed on by other specialties. Those same specialists, however, may argue that quality of care of those procedures can only be assured when the volume is significant, thereby fortifying their own claim to that part of the production turf.

Other factors to consider in multispecialty groups include how the ancillary service revenues will be distributed, which is affected by the interpretation of current Stark law. Another factor will be the variations in malpractice costs by specialty, which may be further compounded by the specific experience of lawsuits within departments.

All these factors point to the reasons why multispecialty practices are perhaps the most challenging to hold together in a coordinated culture. In an ideal situation, the multispecialty group will have worked out their mission, vision and values far in advance of working out the details of compensation plans, and they will use those common foundational agreements as the basis for their discussions. In effect, their reason for being a multispecialty group will serve as an agreement to agree about compensation issues.

Following is an example of how a multispecialty group might allocate overhead by specialty.

Statistics	Total	Prim. Care	Surgeons	Int. Med.	Allocation
Office visits	51,071	44,448	3,749	2,874	
Procedures	83,276	69,305	7,638	6,333	
Square feet	13,450	9,066	3,040	1,344	
Providers	14.00	10.00	3.00	1.00	
Physicians	10.75	6.75	3.00	1.00	
Shareholders	9.00	6.00	2.00	1.00	
Charges	$4,157,340	$2,234,886	$1,622,304	$300,150	
FFS receipts	$2,876,202	$1,747,011	$910,106	$219,085	
Capitation and risk receipts	$607,570	$607,570	$0	$0	
RHC receipts	$103,772	$103,772	$0	$0	
Total Receipts	$3,587,544	$2,458,353	$910,106	$219,085	
Overhead Expenses					
Support staff salaries	$874,215	$624,439	$187,332	$62,444	providers
Support staff benefits	$175,634	$125,453	$37,636	$12,545	providers
Staff profit sharing	$0	$0	$0	$0	shareholders
Occupancy expense	$225,391	$151,925	$50,943	$22,522	square feet
Supplies	$149,804	$130,377	$10,997	$8,430	visits
General and administrative	$262,442	$187,459	$56,238	$18,746	providers
Taxes	$50,451	$36,036	$10,811	$3,604	providers
Midlevel costs	$249,399	$249,399	$0	$0	direct
Officer compensation	$20,000	$13,333	$4,444	$2,222	shareholders
Total Expenses	$2,007,336	$1,518,422	$358,401	$130,513	
Dept Gain(Loss)	$1,580,208	$939,931	$551,705	$88,572	
Expense per PHYSICIAN	$186,729	$224,951	$119,467	$130,513	
Percent of total expenses	100.0%	75.64%	17.85%	6.5%	
Expense/Receipts	55.95%	61.77%	39.38%	59.57%	

HOSPITAL-OWNED MEDICAL PRACTICES

The relatively brief history of hospital-owned medical practices has been a stormy one. The strategy of acquiring loyal referral bases has backfired for many hospitals. Estimates of annual operating losses for hospital-owned physician practices are still in the five-digit range per physician, although some hospitals have found ways to dilute or neutralize the red ink in their medical practices.

Hospitals that have been more successful in this arena have found physician compensation to be a critical tool, both in its form and its implementation. In their initial enthusiasm to secure loyalties, many hospitals offered market salaries and attractive bonuses without considering the long-term economic consequences to the institution. They quickly discovered that, as the physicians were no longer at risk for their compensation, their motives for producing at former levels also evaporated. While many hospitals have thrown up their hands and elected to get out of the physician practice business, others have found that they can restore win-win relationships through a combination of trust-building and equitable compensation agreements.

Trust-building is the key. If physicians have lost faith in their institution to deal equitably with them, there is almost nothing that can be done in a compensation agreement to restore the trust. Trust has to come first. Once the trust is nourished, invigorated and carefully protected on both sides, physicians have a much better opportunity to buy into the compensation concepts proposed by the hospital, and physician buy-in is the key to their retention.

The most successful long-term hospital-owned practices seem to have found value in insisting that physicians retain a certain degree of risk for their production. It is not unusual to see compensation agreements that place 10 to 20 percent or more of total physician compensation at risk for meeting or exceeding production targets. Under those agreements, physicians understand that there is no such thing as a free lunch, even when dealing with the institution that depends on them for admissions. Hospitals, on the other hand, understand that there is no such thing as automatic physician loyalty consummated by an employment agreement. In short, successful hospital-owned practices are those where a balance is struck between the long-term market value of the arrangement and the short-term value of being a high producer.

ACADEMIC SETTINGS

Physician compensation in academic settings is still typically based on production, but production is redefined compared to traditional practices. Clinical performance can still be measured by charges, receipts, relative value units or any number of other measurements, but production in an academic setting also includes two other components: The responsibilities for *teaching* and *research* must be articulated separately from clinical production. Those who have administrative responsibilities may see an additional supplement to their compensation.

The challenge in academic settings is to convert non-clinical activities to a measurement that makes sense in a clinical context. The pediatric department at the University of Michigan found Work RVUs as a foundational measurement tool and converted teaching, administrative and research responsibilities to Work RVU measures. Other academic practices focus on the value of time spent in teaching and research, and the risks and pressures of taking on administrative roles. Performance is still a requirement, but the measures in an academic setting may define it differently from non-academic settings.

RURAL PRACTICES

Physicians in rural practices often find themselves in a condition that is both an opportunity and a dilemma. Their geographic isolation may enable them to make their own rules about how to practice, much as a monopoly might perform. On the other hand, small-town dynamics may not be all that forgiving if a physician does not also behave as an exemplary citizen.

This dynamic between rural physicians and their patients carries over to rural physicians and their medical peers. Even if the peers are all solo practitioners, there is an inescapable interdependence that requires physicians to maintain referrals within the community for the benefit of the entire community. Physicians in rural group practices have to come to terms with that interdependence at a higher level. Not only are they interdependent for referrals and cross-coverage, but they also can't afford to isolate themselves from the tight societal fabric of the small town. The physician who does not comply with peer pressure may be forced to uproot his or her family rather than simply move across town to an alternative practice. If ever there was pressure to form sustainable agreements among physicians on compensation, the rural practice setting is the most challenging.

It is interesting to observe that multispecialty practices seem to thrive best in rural settings. Even the venerable Mayo Clinic grew up in what was once a small rural community of Rochester, Minnesota. The interdependence that holds physicians together in rural settings seems to be related to the interdependence that holds multispecialty groups together. Physicians in relatively isolated communities are keenly aware of what is at stake if they fail to find and adhere to common ground. We may find some of the finest examples of collaboration on physician compensation and other issues in rural, multispecialty practices.

NONPHYSICIAN PROVIDERS

Compensation for nonphysician providers can vary dramatically in accordance with the role they are expected to play. Nonphysician providers include physician assistants, certified nurse practitioners, nurse anesthetists and nurse midwives. The scope of practice of each discipline varies from state to state, but in most states nonphysician providers can provide at least some level of billable services with minimal direct supervision by the employing physician.

Nonphysician providers are deployed in practices in various ways as well. Some providers are used to truly extend the capability of the physician as he or she sees their own panel of patients. In primary care practices, nurse practitioners are often found in patient education roles, which may be less revenue-producing, but may also free up the physician for more intensive services. Nurse anesthetists and nurse midwives are generally prone to function more independently. Their compensation is, therefore, similar to that of fee-for-service physicians.

It is easy for practice managers and physicians to get confused about the role and the financial consequences of nonphysician providers in the practice. Physicians who employ providers in the belief that they'll work as hard as the physician does, but cost less, are generally in for some surprises. When nonphysician providers are placed in the role of urgent care provider, the compensation plan typically takes on a tone of high production. Physicians who employ nonphysician providers, particularly in high managed care situations, need to remain conscientious about the economic consequences of each physician provider's actions.

The experience that seems most prevalent in the field is that nonphysician providers typically are granted a base of between 90 percent and 100 percent of their total potential compensation. This can vary dramatically by the setting, but I think it reflects the confusion about the role as much as it reflects the dynamics of the negotiation.

PART-TIME PHYSICIANS

The challenge of accommodating part-time physicians can be a significant one to compensation formula designers. The growing diversity in the physician workforce is compelling managers and partners to consider alternatives to the one-size-fits-all full-time physician schedule. Husband-wife physician teams are sometimes choosing to share the responsibilities of child rearing and, therefore, share the practice as well. Others choose to follow multiple interests simultaneously, or want to defer full-time commitments until young children are grown.

Each physician's reason for choosing a part-time venue is valid, and medical managers cannot ignore the call for diversity. However, there are several dynamics to consider in designing a compensation formula flexible enough to accommodate part-time physicians. The first factor to consider is what the fixed costs are of employing each physician. Typically, malpractice insurance and rent cannot be reduced if a physician chooses to practice full-time. The practice still requires a commitment to billing technology, phone systems and core staff in sufficient quantity to manage the overall patient flow. Likewise, there are opportunity costs to consider. If space is dedicated to one physician for two days a week and goes unused the remainder of the time, the part-timer's contribution to overhead will be considerably less than a fair share of their cost of overhead. Benefit structures also frequently represent fixed costs when they include insurance plans and annual dues to professional organizations.

The challenge is that, although some costs can be prorated, others can't, and part-time physicians who are going to carry their own weight face a need to produce at a threshold sufficient to cover own fixed and variable costs. If production falls below that threshold, the part-time physician will require supplementation from his or her colleagues in the group. There may be valid reasons a group would follow such a policy, but the sustainability of the circumstance is likely to grow more difficult as fixed costs increase.

The solution for accommodating part-time physicians is to negotiate, to identify the benefits and risks of engaging the person in part-time employment, and to weigh those to determine if there is an overall advantage for the group to consider a part-time solution. The economics and the emotion of each situation often compound each other, particularly if a part-time request is made for a retiring physician or for someone who is partially disabled. The group may want to honor the individual in those circumstances, but honor may come at a price unless the details of a compensation formula are carefully modeled and negotiated.

Following is a model that contends with differences in fixed and variable overhead in an environment with a mixture of fee-for-service and capitation:

Bonus Based on Mixed Model with Fixed and Variable Overhead

				Total
Base salary	$50,000	$75,000	$100,000	
FFS receipts	$160,000	$190,000	$240,000	
Capitation visits	1,000	1,400	1,800	4,200
Percent of cap. visits	23.81%	33.33%	42.86%	
Total HMO revenue				$300,000
HMO revenue applied as percent of visits	$71,429	$100,000	$128,571	
Total revenue	$231,429	$290,000	$368,571	
Contribution to group	$181,429	$215,000	$268,571	
Fixed overhead	$180,000	$180,000	$180,000	
Variable overhead	$10,000	$20,000	$25,000	
Total overhead	$190,000	$200,000	$205,000	
Excess	($8,571)	$15,000	$63,571	$70,000
Bonus share (adj. percent of excess cont.)	0.0%	19.09%	80.91%	

Set base salaries at 75 percent of last year's total compensation.
Apply total HMO revenue (capitation and risk) as percent of HMO visits.
Add applied HMO revenue to net FFS revenue to determine contribution to group.
Subtract fixed and variable overhead to determine total individual overhead.
Split year-end cash as percent of contribution to the group among stockholders.
Forgive negative excesses as long as contribution is at least 90 percent of baseline.
Additional discretionary stipends can be granted to office-holders if corporate goals
are met.

OFFICER COMPENSATION

Administration and medical management requirements grow as groups grow. As groups approach the range of five to ten providers, they often find that consensus governance no longer is efficient for staying abreast of market changes and technology challenges. Non-physician managers, of course, play a vital role in groups at that size, but they cannot substitute for critical governance or physician-to-physician issues.

As groups reach the size where consensus is no longer efficient, they find that the role of elected officers becomes more critical, to assure smooth functioning of the group. The time and decisions required to perform the role well often call for some compensation, at least to offset the production losses of the physician who devotes himself or herself to administration. At the entry level, we typically see compensation arrangements consisting of a flat fee, which serves as a supplement to the officer's base compensation. As groups grow, the complexity of their formulae also grow. The officer remuneration might be represented by the percent of time the officer dedicates to administrative duties. In some groups, officer compensation is tied, at least theoretically, to how well the group performs financially as a whole. As groups reach the size of about two dozen physicians and more, they frequently find that the role has expanded to require a full-time commitment of a medical director at least, and perhaps also of a physician president. There are, of course, a wide variation in titles and roles based on the legal structure of the organization and the internal and external challenges facing the group. As groups grow, however, universally they find the need to engage physicians on a physician-to-physician level and, therefore, devise a level of remunerating them for their efforts.

OPTING OUT OF CALL

Physician compensation systems also need to consider the special needs of the physician who is preparing to retire. Although formal retirement may be a few years away, many delight in the opportunity to extend their career by being taken out of the call schedule. The decision has implications for the individual physician's production, but also for the group's coverage of overhead and the relative satisfaction of a tighter call schedule.

MGMA conducted a questionnaire in 1998 on the topic of arrangements for physicians opting out of call. The range of options was dramatic, from allowing compensation to diminish only as production diminished, to taxing partners as much as 65 percent of their base compensation. The mid-range for the several dozen practices that responded to the questionnaire seemed to be an allowance of about 20 percent of base compensation for the physician who wanted to opt out of call. In other words, their pay would be cut by 20 percent before the rest of the production formula would be applied to the compensation of both the retiring physician and the group as a whole.

Similar negotiations are often the focal point in discussions about hospital service, or about opting out of obstetrical deliveries and retaining gynecological surgery only. Each specialty may have its nuances in procedural capabilities and the interests of each physician, and they will need to be negotiated in a similar fashion.

MULTIPLE GENERATIONS

As physicians in small groups prepare to retire, their strategy often includes recruitment of the next generation to prepare an orderly transition. In small practices, these dynamics can be problematic for physician compensation discussions. The reason they can be problematic is because retiring physicians often feel deserving of compensation that reflects goodwill built up over years of diligent practice. They may seek homage in various forms, including beneficial compensation that grants some special exceptions to the formula deployed for the group as a whole.

These can be emotionally challenging discussions, as in the case of part-time physicians, but I encourage practices in this circumstance to segregate the goodwill value from the compensation discussions. If goodwill is indeed evident and documented, the partners in multiple-generation practices should articulate a method for compensating outgoing honorees for goodwill, but retain production as the core for compensation decisions.

CONCLUSION

When dealing with medical groups on compensation issues, it is not uncommon to hear creative ways that each group manages to assert how it is different from any other practice. The implication of such an assertion is that the medians don't apply, or that the rules of fairness somehow deserve reconfiguration for the benefit of the speaker. As we have seen in this chapter, the diversity of settings can be extraordinarily broad, but the principles of fairness and equity will continue to be the design foundations for compensation plans in every group that wants to be sustainable.

8

The ABCs of Gainsharing
Lessons from the Scanlon Plan
PAUL W. DAVIS AND MAJEL C. MAES

Editor's note: Gainsharing concepts may be more relevant to employees than to physicians, but the interdependence of employee productivity and physician profitability is clear.

WHY GAINSHARING?

Today there is increased interest in gainsharing, a management concept that has endured for more than a century. Gainsharing is a guiding management philosophy of at least five organizations that have been featured as one of the "100 Best Companies to Work For in America." Donnelly Corporation, Herman Miller, Beth Israel Hospital, Motorola, and Dana have all credited at least part of their world-class performance to their gainsharing systems.[13] A comprehensive study conducted by the American Compensation Association (ACA) beginning in 1989 and published in 1994, found companies averaged over $2,410 per employee per year in productivity and quality improvements after installing gainsharing. Subsequent ACA research has confirmed the initial findings. After deducting program expenses, and after paying bonuses of 4 to 5 percent (median) of base pay per employee per year, they received a 222 percent return on every dollar paid out.[14] The financial results are impressive, yet they are only one of the many benefits of gainsharing. Study after study has found that gainsharing programs also improve employee involvement, communication, teamwork, labor relations, and quality.[15] A 1998 study entitled "Participation, Achievement, Rewards—Creating the Infrastructure For Managing Continuous Improvement ("PAR")" conducted by the Work In America Institute concluded that "gainsharing, based on a participative work system . . . strengthens the link between pay and performance and mobilizes everyone in the organization to work toward common goals. It can motivate levels of commitment and achievement that are vital to continuous improvement but that cannot be achieved through traditional merit pay systems."[16]

The renewed interest in such an old concept can be attributed to pressures that organizations are now facing. In the health care industry as well as every other industry, cost-cutting, layoffs and mergers are considered par for the course. As companies downsize, they seek ways to motivate the remaining employees. As they become flatter and leaner, the old methods of compensation (number of direct reports, etc.) are no longer effective. As competitive pressures increase, they seek ways to increase productivity and quality. After adopting Total Quality Management (TQM) practices, they seek ways to reward and coordinate teams. Unable to afford the high cost of adversarial relationships and ever-increasing base wages, union and management leaders look to gainsharing as a way to encourage cooperation within collective bargaining.

Although modern gainsharing began in manufacturing, the concepts can be applied to nearly any organization. The medical field is only beginning to experiment with this type of incentive system. In a 1999 health care profession Information Exchange Questionnaire on Employee Incentive Plans conducted by the Medical Group Management Association (MGMA), only 55 of the 387 groups surveyed had a group incentive system in place. Nearly all were profit-sharing plans. Of those 55, most programs were too young to gauge their success rate. However, indications that things were being learned from the profit-sharing initiatives were reflected by comments that ranged from "most employees are not motivated by money" to "staff is now very in tune to excess costs[17]".

THE CROW AND THE CORMORANT REVISITED, OR "WHAT IS GAINSHARING?"

The Japanese have a fable about a crow and a cormorant. In this ancient tale a crow admires the cormorant, a black water bird that can swim in order to catch fish. The crow reasons that because he is a black bird like the cormorant, he too should be able to swim, so he dives into the water only to drown. The fable's lesson is that things that appear to be the same may not be, due to subtle, obscure differences. Those interested in gainsharing should remember the crow's experience, because gainsharing systems that at first appear to be identical reveal fundamental differences upon closer scrutiny.

Gainsharing is a generic term with widely different definitions. For many, gainsharing is simply a group bonus calculation. For others, gainsharing describes a very sophisticated organizational development strategy. For the purpose of this article, the term "gainsharing" will describe any organizational process designed to increase productivity, quality and financial performance by sharing "rewards" with groups of employees. Furthermore, it will refer to practices that include (1) the establishment of specific goals, targets or baselines; (2) the communication to a group of employees of these goals, targets or baselines; and (3) the sharing of rewards when the goals, targets or baselines are exceeded.

This operational definition of gainsharing will not include discretionary management "bonus" practices such as an annual Christmas bonus, because they are not tied to the specific performance of the company. In addition, it will not include individual piecework or merit systems, since they reward individuals and not groups. However, profit-sharing will be considered a form of gainsharing.

THE ABCs OF GAINSHARING

Most of what is written about gainsharing concerns the mechanics of bonus formulas, because various gainsharing systems are typically classified by how the bonus formula is constructed. In these articles Scanlon Plans, Multicost Scanlon Plans, Rucker Plans®, Improshare®, Profit Sharing, and the like are reduced to a paragraph that only an accountant could love. ***While the formula is important for gainsharing success, it is only one factor among many that differentiate the various approaches***. Recent research indicates bonus formulas may not be the most important factors in gainsharing success.[18] A 1998 American Compensation Association study conducted by the Consortium for Alternative Reward Strategies (CARS) produced these major findings:

1. Differences in plan implementation and support drive effectiveness nearly twice as much as differences in plan design.

2. The strongest driver of culture that supports plan effectiveness is the [general] manager, and through his/her example, the direct supervisors of people.

3. What separates the effective and ineffective plans is how well employees understand the details of the measurements, and what they can do to influence them.

4. How much people think about the plan is a key indicator of effectiveness.

5. Companies are missing the boat by not providing recognition as a part of the Group Incentive plan.[19]

In addition, almost all articles written about the Scanlon Plan's bonus calculation since the 1960s are misleading in documenting Scanlon evolution. They have not kept up with current Scanlon theory or application. While they are valuable as history, they provide little insight for those interested in the current state of the art in gainsharing.

The final reason why the formula approach to describing gainsharing is no longer effective is because it describes fewer and fewer gainsharing applications. Historically, gainsharing plans were one-size-fits-all, developed by consultants who trademarked their approaches. Improshare and Rucker are two of the most well known. While Improshare Plans are still being installed, the Rucker Plan did not survive long after the death of its creator. Today, there are still consultants trying to trademark their approaches but most gainsharing systems are customized to the unique needs of each organization.

A new method of classifying the various gainsharing approaches is needed if the reader truly wants to understand the critical differences and make an informed choice. This article will attempt to help the reader understand the ABCs of gainsharing. This simple device, where A= Assumptions, B=Business Literacy, and C=Commitment, will help readers understand which gainsharing approach is right for them. If the ABCs can be mastered, the rest of gainsharing (including designing the bonus formula) will be easier. Because there are only two classic approaches that have survived the test of time, Scanlon and Improshare, they will be used to highlight differences in philosophy and application.

A=Assumptions

All gainsharing systems are developed for some desired end. Typically the motivation may be to produce greater profits, to produce higher quality, or to encourage labor-management cooperation. At the heart of every gainsharing system are assumptions about human motivation and behavior at work. *Gainsharing systems take on specific characteristic based on the assumptions of those who lead, design, and operate them.* These assumptions define the program to a much greater extent than does the method of bonus calculation.

B=Business Literacy

All gainsharing systems claim to increase productivity, profits, or performance. Some are based on the idea that the only thing needed to generate these improvements is more financial motivation, while others stress the importance of teaching employees about the business, so that they will know what to improve and how to participate in improving it.

C=Commitment

Gainsharing is a way to change the commitment level of people at work. All gainsharing systems attempt to shift commitment from the individual to a group or organization. The various approaches differ in the size of the group and the level of commitment they attempt to create.

A = Assumptions about Human Motivation

Throughout human history, we have sought to harness and control human motivation. We have used a wide range of "motivators" to get people to do what we want. We have used punishment, from slavery to starvation, and we have used rewards, from concubines to precious metals. As society became more civilized, we developed money as the universal form of exchange. With industrialization, we developed a wage system where people work for money that they can then use to purchase desired goods and services.

Despite thousands of years of experimentation, there is still great disagreement about what does and does not motivate. Since motivation is the primary reason organizations install gainsharing, the debate is not academic. Research has produced results that at times seem to contradict what most of us assume is common sense. For example, we have learned through research that money may not be as powerful a motivator as non-monetary rewards. Psychologists have attempted to unwrap the mystery of human motivation, yet there are still wide differences of opinion on (1) whether one human being can motivate another: is motivation intrinsic or extrinsic; (2) what motivates people at work; (3) what is the best way for managers to motivate workers; and (4) is money the universal motivator?

Can One Human Being Motivate Another?

All gainsharing systems use some form of incentive or financial reward. So, like the crow, we might assume that all gainsharing philosophies believe deeply in the power of extrinsic motivation. They do not. Scanlon Plans place more of an emphasis on the intrinsic motivation created by participation and education rather than on the extrinsic motivation created by money. Improshare Plans place more of an emphasis on extrinsic motivation. Alfie Kohn, author of *Punished by Rewards: The Trouble with Gold Stars Incentive Plans A's Praise, and Other Bribes,* argues that the only thing accomplished when we try to motivate others is to destroy the intrinsic motivation in each of us. He quotes one of the foremost management scholars and researchers on human motivation, Frederick Herzberg, who said:

> Managers do not motivate employees by giving them higher wages, more benefits or new status symbols. Rather employees are motivated by their own inherent need to succeed at a challenging task. The manager's job then, is not to motivate people to get them to achieve; instead, the manager should provide opportunities for people to achieve so they will become motivated.[20]

Herzberg said this about the typical manager's common sense approach to motivation:

> Managements have always looked at man as an animal to be manipulated with a carrot and a stick. They found that when a man hurts, he will move to avoid pain—and they say, "We're motivating the employees." Hell, you're not motivating them, you're moving them.[21]

What Motivates People at Work?

Researchers and management scholars believe that we each have different needs and, therefore, different motivators. Abraham Maslow predicted that human beings fulfill their needs in a certain order. First, they have a need to eat, sleep, and breathe. He called these physiological needs. When these needs are met, he predicted people would seek to have their security and safety needs met. Maslow believed physiological needs, security, and safety are lower-order needs. When these needs are met, people seek to have their social or affiliation needs met. Next they strive to have their esteem or ego needs met. When all the other needs are met, people seek self-actualization or self-fulfillment. Maslow believed social needs, esteem needs, and self-actualization needs were higher-order needs. Lower-order needs have more to do with our bodies; higher-order needs are related more to our minds.

Frederick Herzberg's work on motivation found that what motivates people is different from what turns them off. He found that working conditions, salary, benefits, status, and security were not motivators. He called them "hygiene factors," and realized they were similar to Maslow's lower-order needs. While they have the capacity to turn people off, they have little capacity to turn people on. Hygiene factors are a base from which the higher-order needs can be addressed. The "motivators" he discovered were responsibility, achievement, recognition, and satisfaction in the work itself. These he realized were related to Maslow's higher-order needs. Luanne Selk, director of training at Beth Israel, put it this way: "My experience is that doctors are generally motivated by the same needs we all have. Like others, doctors respond well when they feel personally valued, and they want to know that someone cares about what they think."

Herzberg's research indicates that if we want to motivate workers, we must first make sure that we have a base to work from. The Work In America Institute "PAR" study agrees: "High levels of performance derived from genuine employee participation generate increased employment stability, which further motivates increasing levels of performance excellence."[22] We must create security by driving out fear, providing insurance, and so on. We must provide adequate salary so the need for food and shelter can be met. Once this base is in place, we can help to provide "motivators" by creating organizations that allow the higher-order needs for affiliation, esteem, responsibility, recognition, and self-fulfillment to be met.

Managers who accept Herzberg's research would create as part of any gainsharing approach opportunities for employees to have their social needs met (perhaps by having them work in teams). They would design their gainsharing system to encourage responsibility and recognition. They would make sure that everyone has a chance for meaningful achievement at work. They would be careful not to use gainsharing to create greater insecurity (by putting pay at risk). They would not view money as a motivator.

What Can Managers Do to Motivate?

There has been some controversy over which management style—"human relations oriented" or "task oriented"—is more effective. The former focuses on people, the latter on production. As Dr. Thomas Gordon, Nobel Peace Prize nominee and author of *Leadership Effectiveness Training,* has found:

> The research clearly shows that the effective leader must be both a "human relations specialist" and a "task specialist". Leader effectiveness requires treating people decently, while at the same time successfully motivating them toward high performance in their work. One without the other doesn't work.[23]

As researchers have explored human motivation at work, they have also studied and written about the nature of management, trying to discover what a manager should or should not do to increase the motivation of the workforce. Managers' assumptions about the nature of people at work have tremendous impact on how they attempt to motivate others. For example, one organization that was exploring gainsharing decided not to pursue the idea further when the president of the organization said, "I do not believe in gainsharing. I grew up in the Depression. Having a job is the only gain anyone needs." He assumed his workforce shared his views. He believed that their need for security would produce motivation. He clung to his assumptions, even though most of his workforce was younger and had never experienced the Depression. He clung to his assumptions even though they are not supported by Herzberg's research.

Managers' assumptions are also influenced by the predominant management gurus of their time. Recent management thought has often been dominated by the work of W. Edwards Deming, Tom Peters and Stephen Covey. These writers stress the importance of employee involvement and participatory management. However, other writers and other philosophies that do not place a value on employee involvement and participation have influenced many of today's practicing managers. These philosophies are in conflict with current management, but are not yet outmoded. Frequently they rely on punishment and rewards as the primary motivators at work.

There are those who still follow the theories of Frederick Taylor, one of the earliest and most influential writers about the role of management. Some even credit Taylor with coining the term "gainsharing." His book, *The Principles of Scientific Management,* written in the early 1900s, influenced a generation of managers and launched industrial engineering as a profession. The book explains how to use the principles of scientific management to motivate a steelworker to work harder by offering him more money for loading pig iron. He illustrates with an actual quotation from a conversation he had with the steelworker:

> . . . you will do exactly as this man (manager) tells you tomorrow, from morning till night. When he tells you to pick up a pig and walk, you pick it up and you walk, and when he tells you to sit down and rest, you sit down. You do that straight through the day. And what's more no backtalk. Now a high-priced man does just what he is told to do and no backtalk. Do you understand that? When the man tells you to walk, you walk, when he tells you to sit down, you sit down, and you don't talk back to him. [24]

Scientific management assumes that some people in an organization are better at thinking, while others should simply do what they are told (without talking back). Money and punishment are seen as the most powerful motivators. Workers are viewed as lazy and unwilling to do their best without management intervention. It is assumed that the average worker does not seek more responsibility, and in fact will avoid responsibility. Douglas McGregor, the great scholar of organizations, would many years later call these assumptions "Theory X."

Management assumptions are critical to gainsharing success. Assumptions are like lenses in a pair of glasses. They will distort, focus, and alter everything a manager sees. A small Michigan manufacturing company was purchased by a group of investors who had experience with the Scanlon gainsharing system. The investors specialized in turnaround situations. The investors' assumptions about management were not "Theory X." The gainsharing approach they selected was highly participatory, and involved the union and the employees in solving company problems. Within three years the company was highly profitable, having carved out a niche by competing head-to-head with the much larger 3M Corporation. The company became so successful that the investors decided to sell, receiving ten times a return on their investment. The Theory X purchasers did not believe in the value of participatory management. Their assumptions distorted their view of the gainsharing system. They saw the bonuses as giving away some of their profits. They saw the frequent meetings required for participation as a waste of time and as a loss of their management power. Within two years, the gainsharing system was in ruins, employee morale was at an all-time low, and the new owners were debating moving the plant south to avoid their union.

Today "Taylorism" has fallen out of favor, but its basic assumptions continue to drive many management actions. Theory X managers usually do not support gainsharing if there is an employee involvement component, yet they may embrace gainsharing as a compensation approach. They tend to support gainsharing systems where pay is at risk. In these systems employees are not paid a market wage, but are able to reach market rates or above with the addition of a gainsharing bonus. These assumptions are the same assumptions that drove the Taylor's piecework systems in the early 1900s. The assumptions driving these systems are that money is the primary motivator, and employees will not work hard unless their paycheck is at risk. They assume people do not want to work. They believe management must intervene by designing a more effective carrot if workers are to be motivated to work.

While McGregor studied managers with Theory X assumptions, he also studied managers with quite the opposite assumptions about people. McGregor called these assumptions "Theory Y." These managers assume that workers want to accept more responsibility, actually enjoy work, want to set their own goals, have great ambition, and can be trusted. Today, most modern management practices such as TQM, Teams, Employee Involvement, and so on are based on Theory Y assumptions. Few managers realize that McGregor developed Theory Y by studying a variety of organizations with Scanlon gainsharing systems. McGregor endorsed Scanlon by saying, "I need only mention the Scanlon (gainsharing) Plan as the outstanding embodiment of these ideas in practice." Donnelly Corporation, a world leader in the automotive glass industry, has had a Scanlon gainsharing system since 1952. Often ranked as one of America's most admired corporations, the company has been a leader in

Theory Y management practices. Donnelly CEO Dwane Baumgardner, considered to be one of the top 36 business leaders in America,[25] describes the essence of Theory Y management:

> True motivation . . . is an internal drive that is released by a commitment to worthwhile goals. We believe that everyone has a deep internal desire to have their life make a difference, and they want to be part of a worthwhile endeavor. People will willingly and energetically work creatively toward organizational goals if they believe them to be worthwhile.[26]

Baumgardner goes on to say:

> I believe a strong distinction should be made between incentives and motivation. Incentives encourage people to concentrate on the reward, not the work to be done. They encourage many nonproductive behaviors. We believe at Donnelly that pay in and of itself is not a strong motivator, but can be a de-motivator.[27]

Is Money the Universal Motivator?

The assumptions behind the Scanlon gainsharing system are congruent with the work of McGregor, Maslow and Herzberg. Scanlon Systems are based on the assumption that people want to participate and accept responsibility. Other gainsharing systems were developed based on different assumptions about human motivation. Mitchell Fein, the creator of the Improshare gainsharing, wrote:

> Herzberg's postulation that money is not a motivator, that the work itself motivates, was sweet music to manager's ears. Not only did workers not accept these notions; neither did management. [28]

Fein assumes that money is the primary motivator. While Improshare encourages employee involvement, it is not viewed as the critical component like it is in Scanlon gainsharing systems. Fein cites his own studies, which indicate that the Improshare system motivates and creates greater productivity without the need for employee involvement. The debate has taken on renewed vigor as a result of the work of the late W. Edwards Deming. Deming, the great quality expert, had very strong feelings about motivation and the role of money as a motivator. He believed in the power of intrinsic motivation. He believed that individual merit pay systems, rewards, punishment, and most of the other motivators used in business were dysfunctional. He believed in Theory Y management. Deming summed up over 50 years of organizational study by saying, "Pay is not a motivator."

If pay is not a motivator, why then is it so common? Voltaire said, "When it is a question of money, everybody is of the same religion." Fein writes:

> Money incentives have come to occupy a central place because money is a common means for satisfying all sorts of diverse needs in our society and because money may be handled and measured. Money is "real"; it is communicable. Many other means to need-satisfaction are abstract and ephemeral.[29]

Jerry McAdams, in *The Reward Plan Advantage,* takes a pragmatic approach that seeks the middle ground.[30] He does not take the extreme position of Deming or Kohn that all motivation is intrinsic, nor does he endorse the assumptions of Leavitt and Fein that extrinsic monetary rewards are sufficient motivators alone. He believes that a properly designed reward system will avoid the problems of both extremes. McAdams' credibility is enhanced by the fact that he was head researcher in several large-scale studies of alternative reward systems for the American Compensation Association.

Because money is universal, quick and easy, it often becomes the only focus of many gainsharing systems. Gainsharing as compensation or a "bonus" is easier to design, communicate, and administer than is a more comprehensive method such as Scanlon. However, Scanlon practitioners have found the real value of financial rewards isn't the money they provide per se, but the way the money helps to focus employees and management on business issues. Scanlon practitioners no longer view Scanlon as simple gainsharing, as a plan, or as a program. They consider Scanlon to be a *process* for organizational and individual development. Each part of the process is important for success. They believe most gainsharing systems have fatal flaws built into them. Typical gainsharing approaches that consider money to be the only motivator can only motivate when there are bonuses to be paid. They do not provide motivation during tough times, when a company can't pay bonuses but needs motivated employees the most. Many operate much like a lottery. Employees enjoy the opportunity to earn extra money but they believe the bonus is subject to chance. They do not believe they can influence the results. The focus on gainsharing as a program or a plan, instead of a *process* or *system,* prevents them for adapting and changing which creates built in obsolescence.

There appears to be a basic paradox among gainsharing practitioners. Gainsharing is viewed as a solution for motivating workers by managers who have totally opposite assumptions about what motivates them. Each camp has its own management theorists to justify its assumptions. Each is able to cite objective studies to validate its position. All gainsharing systems are not created equal. Those exploring gainsharing must first determine their own basic assumptions about human motivation and then design a gainsharing process based on those assumptions. If they work with an existing gainsharing process or gainsharing consultant, they must question whether or not the process and the consultant share the same assumptions.

When management assumptions and gainsharing systems match, there is power, synergy and integrity. Gainsharing becomes a way for the manager to manage. When management assumptions and gainsharing don't match, gainsharing is not effective. Gainsharing sends a strong message to the organization about what behaviors are important. Employees are quick to find inconsistencies between what the managers say and what gainsharing rewards. While this is not to say that consistency per se makes gainsharing successful, inconsistencies will soon undermine even the best gainsharing process.

The following questions and/or suggestions are designed to help you explore your assumptions and determine what gainsharing approach is congruent with your assumptions. Since Scanlon and Improshare are the only classic approaches still being installed, they are highlighted. If the reader is evaluating another approach or designing a generic gainsharing process, use the questions to help clarify your thinking.

Questions to Consider: Assumptions

1. Do you believe workers are motivated more by extrinsic rewards or intrinsic rewards?

   - If extrinsic, design a gainsharing process that focuses on money as a motivator. Consider Improshare.
   - If intrinsic, maybe you should not even consider gainsharing. If you do, consider a process that takes into consideration intrinsic motivators like participation. Consider Scanlon.

2. Do you agree with Herzberg that the human motivators are responsibility, achievement, recognition, and satisfaction with the work itself?

- If yes, build your plan to include these motivators. Consider Scanlon.

- If no, what do you believe are the needs of your workforce? If you believe money is a universal need, design a process with a large bonus component. Consider Improshare.

3. Do you believe in Theory X or Theory Y management?

- If X, consider scientific management. Consider designing a piecework system instead of gainsharing. Consider automation or contracting out as a way to increase productivity and quality. Consider putting a large part of your employees' wages at risk. Consider a merit system instead of a gainsharing system.

- If Y, involve your employees in designing the process. Do not use money as the only source of motivation. Use gainsharing to build participation and commitment. Include all employees in the gainsharing pool. Consider Scanlon.

B=Business Literacy

One of the hottest management ideas of the late 1990s is the idea of Business Literacy or "open book management." Authors such as John Case, Jack Stack, and John Schuster have done a wonderful job of documenting the effects literacy training has had on a wide variety of organizations. Stack's own organization, Springfield Remanufacturing Corporation, has become one of the most sought-after places for a benchmark visit because of its amazing turnaround story.

What these open book managers and/or authors have discovered is the power generated when employees know their business, are provided meaningful information on the performance of their business, are able to influence decisions to improve their business, and are included in the rewards of capitalism. Open book practitioners seek to create companies where every employee is a business-person.

Despite the hype, these ideas are not new. Many were developed over half a century ago by Joe Scanlon, the father of gainsharing, and are incorporated in every Scanlon gainsharing process. Joe was an eclectic man. During his lifetime he was a steelworker, union leader, cost accountant, prizefighter, researcher, and lecturer at the Massachusetts Institute of Technology (MIT.) His name has become synonymous with gainsharing.

During the Depression Joe learned the value of cooperation by helping unemployed steelworkers find land and seed for gardens. After the Depression, he found himself on the union bargaining committee in negotiations with his employer, Empire Sheet and Tube. Barely profitable, Empire was not able to increase wages and was in danger of going under. In desperation, Joe sought advice from the International Brotherhood of Steelworkers. He was told to return to Empire to see if there was any way the workers could improve the company in hope of making it more profitable. The workers had many ideas for improving the company, and Empire was saved. News of Joe's work spread and soon he was helping other workers and their companies cooperate to survive.

The initial Scanlon plans had no "gainsharing" bonus formula. They focused on business literacy and employee involvement. As companies became stronger and survival was no longer the issue, the idea of sharing gains was born. The initial gainsharing formulas were designed to share improvements in labor productivity. As workers were able to reduce the cost of labor, these savings were split, with 25 percent of the savings going to the company and 75 percent going to the workers. The plans were very successful. Joe was asked to join the Steelworkers Research Department. With the outbreak of WWII, Joe became involved in creating joint Union and Management Councils to help with the war effort. After the war, labor and management were no longer interested in cooperation. Joe was asked by Douglas McGregor to join the faculty of MIT, where he was involved in establishing gainsharing systems until his death in 1956. Russell Davenport reported on the philosophy, methods and potential of Scanlon's ideas in "The Greatest Opportunity on Earth" and "Enterprise for Everyman," two *Fortune* Magazine articles in 1949 and 1950.[31, 32] Joe's work was continued by Dr. Carl Frost and Mr. Fred Lesieur. Frost contributed to Scanlon theory and practice by creating the Frost/Scanlon Principles. Lesieur worked with MIT, and specialized in installing Scanlon Plans in companies with unions.

The Scanlon *Process* has survived for over half a century, and many of America's "best" organizations have used Scanlon. Motorola, Herman Miller, Dana, Donnelly, Sears, Magna Copper, Beth Israel Hospital, and Whirlpool are just a few of the organizations influenced by Joe's ideas. Joe never trademarked his process nor copyrighted his ideas, believing they should be made freely available. Today many generic plans (and some trademarked plans) are really Scanlon Plans. Scanlon Plans are a combination of philosophy (Theory Y), principles, and common-sense practices. Reflecting his basic belief in business literacy and employee involvement, Joe wrote:

> What we are trying to say is simply this: That the average worker knows his own job better than anyone else, and that there are a great many things that he could do if he has a complete understanding of the necessary. Given this opportunity of expressing his intelligence and ingenuity, he becomes a more useful and more valuable citizen in any given community or in any industrial operation.[33]

The primary Frost/Scanlon Principle is called *identity*. The principle of identity incorporates what writers are today calling *business literacy*. Through a *process* of education all employees are taught about their company, their competitors, and the need to change. Each Scanlon company develops its own *process* to insure identity. Customer visits, information on competitors, and training on how to read financial reports are all ways that Scanlon companies create identity. Beth Israel Hospital implemented identity by sharing hospital information with its employees in three languages (French, Spanish, and English). Wescast Industries, a Canadian company that produces 60 percent of the engine manifolds in North America, conducts monthly business information meetings and maintains an in-depth company intranet system. Limerick Veterinary Hospital in Limerick, Pennsylvania, created their entire business education process (which they call "P.A.W.S.") using pet themes. Each company designs an identity *process* that fits its industry and size.

Questions to Consider: Business Literacy

1. Do you believe business literacy among all employees in your company/organization is important?

   - If yes, consider developing a gainsharing *process* that stresses the importance of business literacy. This can be done through training, but also through systems that encourage business literacy, i.e., screening committees, BIZ-WIZ® or Cash Flow

Chronicles™ programs, etc. Include developing business literacy as part of the installation strategy of your *process*. Consider Scanlon.

- If no, focus your system on the financial reward potential of gainsharing. Consider Improshare.

2. Are you willing to share financial and operational data with your employees?

- If yes, read the open book management literature for ideas on how to do this. Consider Scanlon.

- If no, business literacy is not for you! Scanlon is not for you.

C=Commitment

Organizations are changing their commitments to customers, investors and employees. The quality movement has helped world class organizations increase their commitment to customers. Investors led by the large institutions have demanded and received increased commitment to their needs. Paradoxically, during these times of increased commitment to customers and investors, organizations are decreasing their commitment to employees. Many employees work part-time, their organizations unable or unwilling to commit to full-time employment. Full-time employees are told it is impossible for their organizations to commit to lifetime employment. Organizations that have become flatter and leaner cannot even commit to regular advancement for good performers.

While employees are told to expect less organizational commitment, they are asked to commit to new forms of work. They are asked to commit to longer hours and more responsibility. They are expected to commit to being flexible. They are told to commit to lifetime learning to master ever more complex and changing jobs.

Albert Camus said, "Commitment is the soul of work." Johann Goethe said, "Until one is committed, there is hesitancy, the chance to draw back, always ineffectiveness, concerning all acts of initiative (and creation). There is one elementary truth the ignorance of which kills countless ideas and splendid plans: That the moment one definitely commits oneself, then providence moves too."

The various gainsharing approaches differ in the commitment they make and the commitment they seek. Those that are implemented as a compensation strategy commit to pay a bonus when certain performance targets are met. This, in and of itself, is a major commitment, just like a commitment to meet payroll, to fund benefits, and so on. Once an organization commits to gainsharing, it must follow through with the commitment. A bonus cannot be promised and then withdrawn later. Most gainsharing systems are self-funding, paying for their administration and the bonuses out of gains or savings, yet even these systems demand organizational commitment. For example, Lincoln Electric had to borrow money to meet bonus commitments. Their system paid a bonus based on productivity gains. Employees improved productivity, yet the company was not profitable. This doesn't happen often, but it does illustrate the point that a commitment to a bonus is a commitment that must be honored in good times and bad. Many companies avoid that particular scenario by establishing a nominal baseline profit margin, which the company must meet or exceed before any bonus is paid out.

Gainsharing systems such as Scanlon that are (fundamentally) organizational and individual development systems, demand great commitment from employees and their organizations. They demand personal and organizational commitment to participation, to equity, and to increased competency.

Commitment to Participation

Every gainsharing system seeks to alter the commitment of individuals. As a result of gainsharing, individuals are assumed to participate in some way to making the group or organization better. The various approaches differ on how widely to encourage participation and on who is included in the gainsharing group. Some focus only on the production people in an organization, and do not include administrative people or managers. Some focus on teams, with each team operating its own bonus system. Some focus on multiple plants or sites. Gainsharing writers call this the "line of sight" issue. People want to be able to influence the results of a bonus. Creating line of sight is a fundamental way of emphasizing the link between performance and reward. It leads clearly from employees' behaviors to achievement, measures them against specific goals, and then uses these measures to determine payoff.[34] The more people are involved, the more difficult this becomes. The less a bonus measure is influenced by participation, the harder it is to explain and to enlist support. For example, employees in a manufacturing operation might feel that they can participate in reducing scrap, yet they may feel they have no control over profits (even though the two measures are related).

The question of whom to include in the gainsharing group becomes a question of philosophy and pragmatism. The Scanlon philosophy is to include as many as possible. Thus, all levels and jobs are usually identified as participants. This creates "we are all in it together" thinking. It makes it easier for departments and teams to work together, since they share the same Scanlon bonus. It allows white-collar and blue-collar workers to find common ground. In larger organizations such as Wescast Industries, each facility develops its own gainsharing system based on its specific needs. This arrangement fits Wescast's organizational structure and allows for a manageable size. In smaller organizations, the group may be defined as the entire organization. Sometimes even part-time employees and key vendors are included in the *process*.

Commitment to participation can be built into gainsharing or it can be left to chance. For example, historically the Scanlon approach encourages participation through a suggestion system and committee structure. Employees submit suggestions to a production committee made up of coworkers and managers, who then decide whether or not to implement the suggestions. Production committees are workgroup- or department-based. Production committees send representatives to a screening committee made up of top management and union leaders. The screening committee reviews suggestions that were rejected and those suggestions that involve multiple departments or large expenditures of money to implement. This system exists in many organizations as well as some newer forms of participation such as work teams and Kaizan teams.

Employees in Scanlon companies are expected to participate by "influencing decisions in their areas of competence." The commitment to participation is evident in the way the Scanlon process is implemented. Scanlon is not purchased off-the-shelf from consultants or third parties. They are not implemented unless there is evidence of virtually universal organizational commitment at all levels. The process, begins with discussions at the top level of the organization. Every top leader, after learning about the Scanlon process, is asked to make a personal and professional commitment of support. Only when the top-level team is personally and professionally committed is it introduced to the other levels of the organization. If there is a union, the union leadership is introduced to the idea. Eventually all the levels of management, including the front line supervisors, are introduced to the concepts of Scanlon and asked to make a personal and professional commitment of support. When the managers representing the organization, their departments, and their professions have committed and the union leadership has committed, the process is explained to the rank-and-file employees. They too are asked to commit to creating a different way of working through the Scanlon process. They vote to participate by electing a committee to design the Scanlon system. After it is designed the committee presents its work to all of the employees and a vote to try Scanlon for a trial period is taken. Acceptance levels of 80 to 90 percent are usually required for the process to be implemented. Finally, after the trial period, the Scanlon process is evaluated one more time and a vote is taken to continue Scanlon indefinitely as a way or working together.

This process is time-consuming. It takes on average 35 weeks from initial exploration until Scanlon is approved for the trial period. The process is not designed for speed; it is designed for building commitment and participation. The process creates the following:

1. Commitment: People "own" the process, even giving it a unique name like U.N.I.T.E., Q.U.E.S.T., P.A.R.T.N.E.R., I.C.E., etc.

2. The process does not belong to one department like Human Resources.

3. The process prevents Scanlon from becoming another "flavor of the month" approach.

4. The process requires an organization to spend time up front explaining gainsharing rather than risking people will understand later once it is in place.

5. Every company is unique; the process prevents one-size-fits-all mistakes.

6. The process builds internal competence. A company does not become dependent on consultants or others to maintain or improve the system. Employees grow as human beings as they learn new skills.

7. The process creates the links and support needed for implementation as well as design.

8. The process creates a model that can be used when it needs to be renewed.

9. Success: A study done at the University of Wisconsin found that participation, voting, and plan understanding were highly correlated with gainsharing success.[35]

The idea of employee voting is intimidating to some, especially with an 80 to 90 percent approval rate recommended. However, the vote rarely fails. More typically, as the process unfolds, issues will surface that may require a delay or change in the process. For example, one company decided not to pursue Scanlon because they were involved in ISO certification and the top managers did not feel they could handle both initiatives at the same time. Once ISO was completed, the company began the Scanlon process. Others may decide not to continue because the union will not support gainsharing or the top management team cannot accept Theory Y management practices. The commitment level the process generates is illustrated by what happened in a Sears installation. A long-term employee became sick and was taken to the hospital on the day the vote was to be taken. She called from her hospital bed because she wanted the vote to be unanimous.

Other gainsharing approaches require little commitment to participate from employees. They are designed by internal or external consultants and then simply communicated to employees. They can be installed quickly. There is no vote. They can be changed quickly and easily. They do not create commitment.

The issues surrounding participation and gainsharing are similar to the issues surrounding participation and employee stock ownership plans (ESOPs). Participation is not required for gainsharing, nor is it required for ownership. Participation is linked to the strategy or reason for adopting gainsharing as it is linked to the reasons for adopting ESOPs. Some gainsharing systems are viewed as a compensation strategy, and participation is not required. Some ESOPs are viewed as a tax-saving strategy, and participation is not required. However, research on both gainsharing and employee stock ownership has found that effectiveness is increased when combined with participation.

Questions to Consider: Participation

1. Do you wish to commit to participation?
   - If yes, consider designing participation into the system from the beginning by having employees create the system. Make sure top leadership is committed to making gainsharing a success. Consider Scanlon.
   - If no, Improshare may still require more participation than you feel comfortable with. Do *not* consider Scanlon.
2. Do you have time for participation?
   - If yes, consider a process like Scanlon
   - If no, wait until you have time. You simply cannot have meaningful participation if you don't take the time.

Commitment to Equity

Webster's defines equity as "the quality of being fair or impartial." Scanlon gainsharing systems incorporate this idea of fairness by defining equity as a genuine commitment to accounting for the needs of all constituents including customers, investors and employees. The concept is graphically depicted as an equilateral triangle.

The pursuit of equity is the way the Scanlon gainsharing system holds everyone accountable to the stakeholders. Dwane Baumgardner notes:

> People often think equity means equality, although that is not the case. Others think it mainly means a bonus, and that is not the case. The principle of equity means that, among all of the company's stakeholders, there is a fair return for their investment and all issues are dealt with in a spirit of fairness to all—in short, a focus on "we" vs. "me." Equity is a balance, and the responsibility for attaining balance is a shared responsibility of all the stakeholders.[36]

Scanlon is the only gainsharing process that defines these multiple accountabilities, yet the idea is probably as old as time itself. Confucius was reported to have said, "The proper man understands equity, the small man profits." Equity is important because a focus on only one or two of the stakeholders will ultimately destroy an organization. For example, the auto industry in the U.S. historically has been a good place to work, with high pay and good benefits. It has also been a good place to invest, yet consumers began switching en masse to Japanese automobiles in the 1970s because they were not happy with the quality and service of U.S. companies. We were close to losing the industry until the auto companies and their employees made the gut wrenching changes needed to compete. There are companies whose profitability is unacceptably low or nonexistent, yet employees demand higher and higher wages, eventually forcing the company to go out of business. Today, there are companies that lay off their employees even though they are highly profitable with record sales. The companies are liquidating their human assets and setting in motion their own demise.

Dr. Carl Frost, in describing the Scanlon Equity process, said:

> During the early days of Scanlon and somewhat persistently since, many have defined equity as bonuses. The early days were adversarial. Wages were not nationally uniform or substantial. Too often management permitted and even encouraged the expectation of supplemental income, primarily as a result of productivity improvements, i.e., Improshare, gainsharing. The use of the word *share* often suggests difference and division rather than neutrality of benefits that are mutually inclusive rather than exclusive.[37]

Scanlon companies make the equity concept operational by creating appropriate reliable databases of customer satisfaction, financial performance, and human resources. There are regular, public occasions where the data is shared and discrepancies between what "is" and what "needs to be" are explored. Sometimes, positive discrepancies are noted and sometimes negative discrepancies are found. Frequently, bonus formulas are constructed that take into account the needs of all stakeholders. Spring Engineering and Manufacturing Company even named their Scanlon system the I.C.E. Plan for *Investor*, *Customer*, and *Employees*, to emphasize equity. The Scanlon Equity Principle includes many concepts business writers are now calling a "balanced scorecard."

Bonus formulas that take into account the needs of all stakeholders are better than those that emphasize only one. The Lincoln Electric bonus, mentioned earlier, might satisfy employees but may not meet the needs of investors. One company paid a bonus to employees for improvement in quality, yet the firm's customers said the company's quality standards were too low. The company found itself rewarding employees for performance that its customers would not accept. These examples illustrate the difficulty in creating equity. It is much easier to simply create a bonus. However, an equity system is superior to a bonus system alone, because equity provides the greatest long-term organizational security. Scanlon gainsharing experience has found that the primary reason employees are interested in developing a Scanlon process is to provide long-term employment security and not to provide short-term bonuses.

Companies that stress a bonus create employees who are dissatisfied when the bonus cannot be paid. These employees are conditioned to expect a bonus. They are not literate to the fact that their investors may be losing money, or that their customers have gone somewhere else. In companies committed to equity, employees know the needs of the other stakeholders and are willing to make sacrifices when necessary. Beth Israel employees, upon discovering that each blood transfusion cost the hospital $200, developed a program to donate their own blood to the center, thus saving the hospital much of that expense. During the recession of the late 1980s, Donnelly paid out no bonus for three years, and yet because management believed that the company treated them like equal partners, they accepted a proposal to cut all salaries above $40,000 from 3 to 17 percent. Donnelly emerged from the recession with a strong and dedicated workforce. In 2001, Spring Engineering & Manufacturing faced their first-ever layoffs, which was a potentially devastating occurrence for this small company. In a spectacular demonstration of employee buy-in, the entire company voted to eliminate their gainsharing bonus in order to save two jobs.

Organizations make the principle of equity operational in many ways. Traditionally, they decide what to measure and then construct a historical baseline that represents the current level of the measure(s). When the measure(s) is exceeded, the gain is split between the company and the employees. Operational measures such as labor productivity, scrap, safety, or quality measures are typical. Financial measures such as profit, ROI, and EVA are also used. American Compensation Association survey results indicate that organizations report greater success with measures that take into account both operational and financial measures.[38] The employees' portion of the gain is placed in a bonus pool and is distributed either on a percentage basis of salary or "hours worked." (The Fair Labor Standards Act regulates how nonexempt employee bonuses are computed and should be consulted before designing a bonus formula.) Almost always the bonus is paid monthly or quarterly. Often a portion of the employees' share is put in a reserve account and used to cover any future deficits. At the end of the year, any remaining reserves are then returned to the employees. The most typical way the bonus is paid is a separate check. These methods have withstood the test of time because they are considered fair and reasonable and are usually not difficult to design and compute.

Increasingly some organizations take a quite different approach. They look *forward* and ask the question, "What performance is needed to achieve our objectives in the upcoming period?" They believe what was adequate in the past may no longer be adequate for the future. They do not wish to reward for improvements if the results still do not meet the continuous improvement goals they have committed to. This system is called goal sharing and it is the approach favored by Sears and Spring Engineering. Both organizations participatively set the goals with their employees so that the employees know the goals are achievable and realistic.

Both the gainsharing and goal-sharing approaches can be used by not-for-profit organizations, although unfortunately there are few examples. One of the best known was Beth Israel Hospital, which had a successful Scanlon system called PREPARE 21. (Their Scanlon system fell victim to their merger with Deaconess Hospital in the late 90s.) While in place, Beth Israel credited its Scanlon process with helping to save hundreds of thousands of dollars in cost, while improving quality and patient care. One of the highlights of Beth Israel's year was the PREPARE 21 Recognition program. During this time, employees and teams were recognized for their contribution to PREPARE 21 and to Beth Israel. It was usually standing room only, when the busy staff of this major teaching hospital came together to honor their own. Recipients not only received the accolades of their peers, but they had their names added permanently to a special kiosk near the hospital's cafeteria.

Other organizations feel that the only true measure of performance is profit and so they develop profit-sharing plans. Purists would argue that profit sharing is a concept foreign to a discussion of gainsharing, but philosophically the ideas are similar. Profit sharing can be considered a financial measure bonus system. Profits above a base number are split with employees. Joe Scanlon studied profit sharing in the 1940s and concluded:

> The analysis of these plans indicates that a sense of participation and partnership is the fundamental prerequisite. If this is fully developed the type of plan itself is of secondary importance. [39]

Douglas Kruse found that profit sharing adoption results in productivity gains of 3.5 to 5 percent.[40]

There are two common challenges associated with profit sharing. The first is a literacy issue. "High performance organizations educate employees in the economics of the business and their industry to put compensation in a broader context and make employees more aware of the ultimate outcomes of their performance."[41] The second issue is the previously mentioned "line of sight." Profit is influenced by many factors beyond the control of the typical employee.

The MGMA Employee Incentive Questionnaire indicates that medical facilities that implement group incentive plans are generally choosing profit sharing and thus could encounter these types of difficulties. However, these challenges are not impossible and there are many successful profit-sharing programs. For example, Wescast Industries combines a once-a-year profit-sharing bonus with a quarterly operational measure bonus system. This system helps to focus employees on the profitability of the corporation, and at the same time on the need for quality, safety, and productivity.

Finally, it is not necessary, and maybe even counterproductive, to give money as the gain. Once a bonus check is cashed and the money spent, it is often difficult for employees to know where the money went. Ferro Corporation—Glass Products Division provides its employees with "mall dollars" that they can spend at local businesses. Employees can purchase goods and services, from vacations to cars. A new electronic gadget may have more "trophy value" than does the equivalent in money. Employees remember what items they received in mall dollars. Enterprising organizations could even use the mall dollar concept to negotiate favorable exchanges and discounts from merchants. An additional benefit of the concept is that money remains in the local economy.

Other examples include Spring Engineering, which was challenged to find a reward system that would recognize great performance in a positive and motivating but low-cost manner. Their ICE Team created a "'Spin the Wheel'" system where a division that has met their monthly goals gets a chance to spin a prize wheel for rewards that range from lotto tickets to leave-early/come-in-late passes. A creative approach was taken by Weyburn-Bartel Incorporated, which paid its bonus in meat. Employees signed up for various cuts of beef or seafood, delivered by refrigerated truck. The system prevented the value of their bonus from being eroded by sales taxes. While these approaches are not for everyone, they show that there are many unique ways to create an equity system.

Questions to Consider: Equity

1. Do you wish to create a bonus system or an equity system?

   - If bonus, consider Improshare.
   - If equity, consider Scanlon. Create a balanced scorecard measuring system. Make sure the bonus formula takes into account the real needs of the stakeholders. Think creatively.

2. Do you wish to do gainsharing, goalsharing or profit sharing?

   - If gainsharing, you will need good historical data from which to create a baseline. Select a baseline period that takes into account your business cycle and typical performance.
   - If goalsharing, you will need to participatively develop goals with employees if you want them to be realistic and accepted.
   - If profit sharing, you will need to determine what measure of profit you will use. You will have to determine what level of profit will result in sharing.

Commitment to Competency

Business literacy, participation, and Theory Y management all require increased employee competency. Employees must learn to do more than what is expected in traditional firms. Motorola's Scanlon philosophy led them to invest over $50 million per year (1990) in employee training and development. Wescast Industries partners with their local community college to offer apprenticeship courses, and will reimburse their employees for these continuing education expenses. Spring Engineering takes it one step further with their Technical Education Academic Manufacturing (TEAM) community college program. TEAM combines applied academic preparation in physics, math, and communication arts with extensive exposure to industry experiences through plant tours, job shadowing, and specialized industry classes. Spring's employees act as mentors and teachers while the students are at their facility. In high-performance work organizations, training also becomes an important component of an employment security strategy.[42] Gainsharing, when utilized as a compensation strategy only, does not identify this type of commitment to increased competency.

Participatory gainsharing requires changes in both managers and employees. Managers must learn how to lead, to listen and to coach. Employees must learn how to work in teams, control quality and reduce costs. Both employees and organizations must commit to major investments in time, energy and money to be successful. Scanlon organizations believe the investment is worth the cost. They believe employees are an asset to be developed and not a cost to be reduced. In three separate audits, Motorola calculated a $30 return for every dollar invested in training and development.

At the very least, every gainsharing system must help employees to become competent in understanding the basis of the gainsharing formula that is used. If employees don't understand the calculation, they will not know why they are or are not receiving the bonus. They will view the bonus as some form of lottery in which they hope to win, but in which they have little influence of the outcomes.

Question to Consider: Competency

> Do you believe employees are an asset to be developed or a cost to be reduced?
>
> - If an asset to be developed, recognize your strategy is for the long term. Consider a Scanlon process.
> - If a cost to be reduced, do not consider gainsharing. Consider reengineering, automation, contracting out or another approach as a strategy.

MECHANICS OF GAINSHARING

Once an organization is clear on the ABCs of gainsharing, the mechanics of gainsharing become more straightforward. It is important to note that Scanlon organizations create their gainsharing systems using a participative design team representing a cross-section of the company. Studies show that design team participation is a critical component to the success of a gainsharing plan. Sears found that employees involved in their Scanlon plan implementation had substantially more favorable responses to the following questions than did employees not directly involved:[43]

SCANLON PLAN

	Participants	Non-Participants
Willingness to make suggestions	67%	48%
Willingness to try to find ways to cut costs	77%	55%
Willingness to seek out information on company performance	60%	37%
Willingness to share in the consequences of company financial setbacks	74%	55%

Every gainsharing system should address the following mechanics before it is implemented.

Questions to Consider: Gainsharing Design

1. What is our reason for considering a gainsharing system, i.e., what do we seek to accomplish?
2. Do we have top management and organization commitment and support?
3. Is this the right time?
   a. Do we have enough time to design the system?
   b. Are there other issues we need to address first?
      i. Management competency
      ii. Union relations
      iii. Compensation system

4. Who will create the system?

    a. Do we work with a consultant?

    b. Do we design it ourselves?

        i. How do we select the design committee(s) and what are their roles?

        ii. How do we involve the organization/union?

5. What are we trying to improve?

    a. How do we measure it?

    b. Do we have all stakeholders identified?

6. Improvement over what?

    a. Gainsharing

        i. How will we construct the base period?

        ii. What is the protection for the company?

            1. Split

            2. Reserve

            3. Caps

    b. Goalsharing

        i. How much money can we spend?

        ii. What are the goals we must accomplish?

        iii. How will we pay out?

    c. Profit-sharing

        i. What measure of profitability will we use?

        ii. How will we protect the company?

            1. Minimum profitability before sharing

            2. Split

            3. Reserves

            4. Caps

7. Who will be covered by gainsharing?

    a. Will we include everybody?

    b. How do we take into consideration line-of-sight?

8. How will we communicate gainsharing to our employees?

9. Who will maintain the system?

    a. Do we need a gainsharing coordinator position?

    b. How do we keep it from becoming another HR Department program?

10. How will we know if gainsharing is successful?

11. How will we change the system?

CONCLUSION

Joe Scanlon believed that the health and success of *any* company depended on its ability to create an environment of cooperation and fairness between labor and management. The best way to achieve that, he felt, was by involving employees in the company and giving them an opportunity to share in the rewards gained through their contributions. Gainsharing is a proven, powerful tool to manage an organization if there is an understanding of the basic ABCs of gainsharing. Mistakes are made by those who do not take the time to understand the differences among the various available approaches. Before beginning a gainsharing program, carefully evaluate your Assumptions about motivation. Consider the impact of Business Literacy. Finally consider the level of Commitment your organization will expect and is willing to provide. Once the basic ABCs are mastered, the right gainsharing approach for you will be much clearer.

MEDICAL PRACTICE EXAMPLES OF GAINSHARING

West Shore Urology in Muskegon, Michigan designed its own limited version of a gainsharing plan, tying employee performance bonuses to peer evaluations. Administrator Diana Schweifler says her staff expressed a desire to have more input to their own evaluations and the performance assessments of each other. She saw this as an opportunity to increase teamwork, and devised a peer review form with 19 questions. Five peers in addition to the administrator/physician leadership team evaluate each employee, with scores given a weighted-average to yield a group consensus about performance. Bonuses are based on the scores within a range established by the physicians.

The incentive system seems to be accomplishing its main goal of building teamwork, although the structure is not specifically tied to the overall profitability of the company. It serves as an example, however, of the principles of gainsharing at work in a medical practice.

A family physician on the East Coast devised a simple method for sharing his gains with his staff. A board in the staff lunch room is updated weekly with a handful of production statistics. When the production tops targeted levels, everyone receives a share of the excess profitability. The board represents a simple method of demonstrating transparency, and encourages all staff members to increase their knowledge and skill to keep the production above the targets.

9

Implementation of Physician Compensation Programs

SETH L. GARBER, MD

Many new physician compensation plans fail at the point of implementation. The costs of failure are high given the investment in the development of such plans, and the damage that can be done to relationships. Accordingly, it is worth exploring some of the more predictable barriers to implementation of physician compensation plans. (Table 1)

INSUFFICIENT MOTIVATION

The implementation of new programs for physician compensation can require great amounts of time, money, and good will. Physicians, management, and analysts involved in designing the new plan will need to commit the time. Not infrequently, significant sums must be spent on information systems to create the databases needed to perform the desired adjustments. Goodwill must be maintained with the physicians. For physicians, the issue of compensation design is not merely one of "How much money will I earn?" but is additionally one of "How much do you value me, and how much do you value what I do relative to what someone else is doing?" Given that these issues touch at the core of the physician's motivation and sense of self-worth, it is essential to have a compelling reason to change the plan in the first place.

The analogy of "the burning platform" is apt: the oil platform must be on fire before one is willing to take a chance on surviving the jump into an icy ocean. Similarly, an

Table 1 Barriers to Successful Implementation

- Insufficient motivation;
- Solving the wrong problem;
- Lack of decision-making process;
- Lack of physician involvement;
- Unclear definitions;
- Misalignment with strategy, payer mix, or policy;
- Inadequate data;
- Too much complexity;
- Failure to model;
- Wrong numbers of utilization of physicians;
- Lack of appeal process;
- Special deals;
- Lack of management controls;
- Failure to measure and communicate success.

organization should not jump into the "icy waters" of a new compensation program for anecdotal or trivial reasons. One or more physicians, for example, may bring in examples from journals that purport to show how much more money his or her peers are making. Without adjusting for local market factors, productivity, and a host of other factors, these comparisons should not motivate one to undertake a full-scale redesign of compensation plans. There are, however, specific "signs and symptoms" of "compensation illness," or sufficient motivation to change compensation design, as shown in Table 2.

Table 2 Potential Signs and Symptoms of Compensation "Illness"

- Significant change in payer mix;
- Increased throughput with decreasing net revenue;
- Difficulty with physician recruiting or retention related to compensation;
- Dysfunctional behavior related to compensation; and
- Severe and real inequities in compensation among physicians with similar productivity.

A significant change in payer mix, which usually means the onset of increasing capitation, may be a signal to re-examine one's compensation system. Obviously, incentivizing visits and procedures in a capitated system will rapidly bankrupt whoever is receiving the capitated payment and carrying the financial risk. While the best time to design the system in theory may be before there are actually any capitated payments (because then nothing is at stake), the implementation of a revised compensation scheme of mixed models, as discussed elsewhere, may best be delayed until the capitated patients and payments actually appear.

A second compelling reason to re-examine and redesign the compensation system may be the phenomenon of increased productivity but with dropping revenue. This can result from a misalignment of what is being defined as "productivity" with what the payor source is rewarding, or, as discussed below, can result from cost structure problems. The latter is not amenable to solution by a change in the compensation program alone, unless that change is simply to reduce all payments to physicians. In this situation, the group must re-evaluate its overhead structure simultaneously with its compensation system.

A third "sufficient motivation" is difficulty in retaining or recruiting physicians, with the key caution that the difficulty must be related to the compensation program if it is going to be solved by the compensation program. Dysfunctional behavior, to the degree that it is caused by a misalignment of financial incentives with the desired behaviors or the payer mix, is another compelling reason to re-examine the compensation plan. Finally, gross compensation inequities (that are real and not simply perceived) among physicians with similar productivity (and similar overhead) are among the most common reasons for a group to seek a new compensation model.

Without one of these compelling reasons to change, communicated to the physicians in a compelling way, the organization may lose interest in traveling the road of implementation when the path becomes rocky. The default position of continuing to do things they way they have always been done will, in such cases, be less threatening and disruptive, and in fact may be more desirable to many in the organization.

SOLVING THE WRONG PROBLEM

Just as a cough can be a symptom of a trivial upper respiratory infection or a symptom of a life-threatening cancer, the "potential symptoms of compensation illness" noted above can be due either to compensation design problems or to other quite different root causes. To attempt to solve the non-compensation problems with a redesign of the compensation assures failure in implementing the compensation plan, as well as failing to solve the real problem. Increased throughput with decreasing net revenue, for example, can also be caused by the underlying cost structure inherent in producing that throughput. The root cause may be poor work design, leading to excess staffing or poor support systems (like medical records availability, order entry, or even physical space limitations) that lead to increasing costs per visit. The solution to these problems lies in redesigning the work flows and the support systems to care for patients more efficiently, not in increasing financial incentives for production. In fact, increasing the incentives will simply add more to the cost per visit.

Difficulties with recruiting are often truly related to the total cash compensation offered, although non-cash benefits are often a consideration, especially to an older physician. Difficulties in recruiting may also be more related to the work environment. The solution, therefore, is to address the perceived ills of that environment, not to further increase the cost structure by front-loading salaries. An additional danger of front-loading physician compensation for recruiting is that physicians will compare their sign-up bonuses or total compensation, leading some to feel under-appreciated. Further, to the degree that the more senior physicians (who are usually the ones in power) see the pay of younger physicians getting very close to their own, they may not accept the implementation of the new compensation design. Finally, a random pattern of recruiting bonuses can lead to a spider-web of "special deals" that may in fact have a discriminatory pattern when viewed as a whole, and can become increasingly difficult to administer in an understandable fashion.

Difficulties with retention are often more directly related to work environment issues than to compensation design. There will certainly be those physicians who will seek a different practice site because they can make more money. To attempt to retain these physicians by changing the compensation plan is self-defeating in a number of ways. First, chances of retaining the physician who has already made a psychological break with the practice are indeed slim. Second, the action of a compensation redesign geared to retention sends powerful message to others who may be considering leaving. Finally, it does not address the root cause of the dissatisfaction. If work life is intolerable at a certain salary, it is not going to get much better for an additional few thousand dollars a year, and the extra money would have been better spent solving the real problems than adding to the fixed cost base.

Finally, there are many "dysfunctional behaviors" not related to compensation issues that will not be solved with compensation redesign. Some organizations, for example, have inquired as to how much of a financial incentive should be built in for the completion of medical records, or for coming to work on time. The expectations around these behaviors are a fundamental part of the definition of work expectations, and should be approached as such rather than as incentive "add-ons." Failure to deal with them are indications of problems in the governance or decision-making processes of the group, and not in the compensation design.

LACK OF A DECISION-MAKING PROCESS

While it is tempting to begin directly with the technical design of the compensation plan, the organization should first ascertain that it has the decision-making processes in place to answer the important questions of design, as well as to implement the new plan. This means being able to answer such questions as "Who will decide? How will we resolve differences? Who has veto power over the new plan?" For multispecialty practices or academic organizations, the questions are even more complicated. "Do all departments have to be the same? Do all clinical chairs need to agree? Will everyone go on the new plan at the same time?" There are no "correct" answers to these questions. What is important is that the organization can map out how these questions will be considered, whether by individuals, standing committees, or ad hoc committees.

Similarly, once the decisions are made, the process for communicating and implementing the changes must also be clear. Who is responsible for communicating the changes? Will appeals be considered? If so, by what mechanism, and to whom?

Unless the practice or organization can map out these processes, the elegant technical solution will remain as one of a collection of three-ring binders on the shelf of the CEO and medical director. For example, one system in the Midwest engaged a consultant over a three-month period to develop an innovative compensation plan with a variable component built around quality and satisfaction measures. The implementation came to an abrupt end when the medical director refused to present the plan to his peers, for fear of his relationship with them. There had been no process in place to assure his buy-in with the plan. In another case, an academic system in the South put together a committee with physician and administrative representation, but did not have an explicit discussion of what their decision-making process would be. After much work, a plan was created, only to have it vetoed by the CFO. A final example was the compensation plan doomed by a well-meaning medical director who had deferred his involvement until the plan was completed and accepted by all. He then put in his changes, only to be surprised by the resistance and ill will that his actions created.

LACK OF PHYSICIAN INVOLVEMENT

A fully developed process for the design and implementation of a compensation plan remains incomplete if there is not sufficient physician involvement. Merely interviewing all the physicians does not constitute "sufficient involvement." While there does not have to be a "Noah's Ark" committee with every specialty represented, a design or advisory group should be put together that is empowered to communicate to and from the various constituencies. The decision-making or advisory authority of this group must also be clear at the outset, just as the physicians at large need to know whether they are providing input or whether they are actually deciding on the design of the plan. Failure to pay attention to the process of gaining involvement invites inevitable serious resistance to implementation of the plan.

UNCLEAR DEFINITIONS

Almost all medical practices would agree that they would like to reward productivity, hard work, excellent service, and good citizenship. Unfortunately, very few compensation committee members will agree on how you define and measure these elements. Productivity, for example, may have different definitions in a fee-for-service as opposed to a fully capitated environment. Some define hard work as how much effort goes in, and others by how much work is produced, regardless of the effort put in. Good citizenship may be service to the medical group, or how well one gets along with other support staff, or something else entirely. The definition must be overt and clear, since someone in the organization is going to have to obtain data for any element chosen as part of the compensation plan to "plug into" the model. Implementation plans have failed when physicians, believing they were to be measured or rewarded by one metric, discover that the actual measurement is of something slightly different.

MISALIGNMENT WITH STRATEGY, PAYER MIX, OR POLICY

A compensation plan, conceived with all the right processes, involvement, and definitions, will fail if it is misaligned with the organization's strategy, payor mix, or policies. Some examples will serve to illustrate. A multispecialty practice owned by an HMO was experiencing difficulties in providing timely appointments to its patients. To reward "access," the compensation plan was modified to provide a small fixed sum of money to the physician for each visit over a certain number per day. In a short time, more visits were indeed being provided. More staff had to be added to deal with the increased traffic through offices, more lab and imaging studies were ordered, and the physicians received more money. Unfortunately, in this case, the HMO and the medical group were fully capitated for the care they provided. This compensation system, for the brief time it was in place, cost them more money for staff and physicians and did not produce a penny more in revenue, because it was misaligned with their payor mix. To further illustrate the problem of unclear definitions, there was no proof that access (defined as a timely appointment with the provider of your choice) was improved for those who needed it.

As another example, one practice wanted to compensate physicians for productivity, which they defined as visits, but paid an incentive for physicians to take night call and be out of the office the next day for physiologic rest. Physicians quickly learned that it was more lucrative to take night call and provide no visits, than to be in the office all day. This mismatch between policy and the compensation system will lead, at best, to failure of the compensation system, and at worst, to confusion and dissatisfaction among the physicians, and to behaviors that may threaten the viability of the practice.

INADEQUATE DATA

The more that the compensation plan moves away from straight salaries, the more data will be needed on productivity by whatever definition one uses. Additionally, many plans are now including variable components around quality, satisfaction, utilization measures, compliance with guidelines, outcomes and citizenship. Defining any of these to the point where one can measure them is a major undertaking. Actually producing the data from existing systems is simply beyond the capacity of many organizations, and innovative plans have stalled at the point where the leadership team moves from "what would we like to build compensation around?" to "what can we actually measure?"

Too Much Complexity

A compensation plan that is too complex will cost more to administer than one that is more straightforward, but more importantly, a plan with a large number of variable incentives may distract from the needed strategic focus of the organization. For example, if the primary need in that practice is to improve access, then a good argument could be made that the first and only variable incentive to be put in place should be around access. If it is clear that access is that the main issue, but rewards are built in for participation in administrative duties and for peer evaluations, the message becomes blurred about what behaviors are most important for the organization. Finally, a plan that is too complex will be hard to communicate to the physicians, and it may be difficult for them to relate their performance to their compensation. If physicians can't understand it, they can't follow in the direction it is pointing.

Failure to Model

Many implementation failures could have been prevented if the effects of the plan had been thoroughly modeled before the plan is implemented. A four-stage modeling scheme has proven effective. First, the prior year's data are used in the model under consideration by the compensation committee. The output is thoroughly reviewed to see if the effects were as desired. In one case, this "dry run" revealed that the more productive physicians in an academic center were going to be disadvantaged by a productivity incentive, while the less productive physicians were going to be rewarded. This anomaly was occurring because the incentive was based on the relationship of production to that portion of the salary coming from the clinical funds (as opposed to grants or other sources), and the determination of how much of one's salary came from clinical sources was an entirely arbitrary one set by the chair of the department. Fortunately in this institution, the modeling revealed the problem before the plan was announced and implemented. It is critical at this point to "gut test" the model before releasing its output to the group at large. One group practice did communicate the first "test" model, which would have erroneously predicted a large drop for one group of specialists. The fact that this was indeed an error was soon thereafter communicated to these specialists, but not before they had all begun searching for other jobs. It is almost impossible to regain the trust of a physician once you have communicated in error that his or her salary is going to drop.

The second stage of modeling, once the accuracy of the data and the suitability of the output has been determined, is to communicate the results to the physicians based on the prior year's data, that is, "Based on last year's data, this is what your pay would have been if this compensation plan had been in effect." Stage three is to produce "phantom checks" on a concurrent basis with actual reimbursement, essentially saying "If this model were in place now, this is how you would be compensated given your current performance." After a few weeks or months of these phantom checks, most physicians are either eager to get on with the new system, or are eager to change their performance to fit optimally with the new system, and full implementation can begin.

An additional advantage of the staged implementation is that it allows the organization to test the production system and makes explicit the multitude of detailed questions relating to data production and compensation adjustments. For example, with variable incentives, will the data be collected every three months, with a time lag to the compensation adjustment, or will it be done on a rolling three-month average? Should the interval be three, six or twelve months for compensation adjustments? Who is in charge of assuring the accuracy of the databases used, and how will the adjustments be computed and fed to the payroll system?

WRONG NUMBERS OR UTILIZATION OF PHYSICIANS

Any effective compensation system must presume that the right numbers of physicians are doing the right things. If this is not the case, a new compensation system will not solve the problem, and further, will probably fail in implementation. One organization, for example, placed a group of primary care physicians in a suburb in anticipation of population growth in that area. The growth, however, occurred in a different area, and those physicians did not become as busy as anticipated. When a new compensation plan that had variable incentives based on production was designed, there was great resentment that these physicians had been "subsidized" by their "harder-working" peers. The compensation system was not at fault, nor were the physicians. The basic problem was that a business investment did not turn out as planned, and therefore needed to be reconsidered (as in moving the physicians to a busier practice location). Another practice was losing money because it was paying a market-based salary to its cardiologists, but they were functioning as internists (and generating the RVUs of internists) because the practice simply did not have enough internists. The ultimate solution to this problem was not in the compensation system, but in staffing the practice appropriately for the needs of its population.

LACK OF AN APPEAL PROCESS

Even the most well constructed and well administered compensation plan will not remain "perfect" forever, and there will be valid reasons for appeal. There must be a mechanism for hearing such appeals and administering them in a consistent fashion, so that precedents can be recognized and so that patterns of unfair discrimination do not arise. Failure to handle such appeals as they come up may lead to a buildup of dissatisfaction that may lead to wholesale and premature rejection of the compensation plan. Many organizations use the same committee that designed the compensation plan to hear and administer subsequent appeals, rather than adding another task to that of line management. In any case, the nature of the appeal and the decision should be well documented.

SPECIAL DEALS

This problem is, in a sense, the opposite of "lack of an appeal process" in that it is the problem of certain individuals having a "special" appeal process. The problem can be historical or contemporary. The historical problem is the web of special deals that frequently grows up in any medical group, whether these deals are prior commitments on hiring, ongoing payments for acquiring a practice, or special assignments of value to certain procedures or activities. When one seeks to produce a rational and equitable compensation system, these deals will surface both to confuse the data obtained and to raise the defenses of the formerly advantaged.

The contemporary problem occurs when certain physicians do not like the way the new compensation system design is heading, and therefore seek a special deal by contract in advance of, or in lieu of, coming under the new system. Allowing that to happen completely undercuts the role and goodwill of the compensation committee and the management team, and makes a mockery of the process.

LACK OF MANAGEMENT CONTROLS

In the absence of other controls, any compensation system may produce untoward (but not unanticipated) results. A production-based system, for example, may lead to over-utilization, an effect moderated by a good utilization review and quality assurance function. A purely capitated system may lead to under-utilization, and special monitors for this phenomenon, including tracking patient satisfaction and outcomes, are necessary management additions to the compensation system. The pure salary model may allow significant discrepancies among physicians in work output or citizenship, issues that must be addressed in the personnel role of management. Without these necessary management monitors, both the compensation system and the entire fabric of the delivery of medical care may be at risk for unraveling. The compensation system alone cannot become a substitute for wise medical management, personnel administration, and leadership.

FAILURE TO MEASURE AND COMMUNICATE SUCCESS

Many compensation systems do not fail dramatically in implementation, but simply wither away from disuse and disinterest. This atrophy stems from the failure of those administering the system to determine and communicate whether the changed compensation system was a success or not. This brings us full circle, to the first section of this chapter, because the definition of success for a compensation plan rests on why the organization embarked on the change in the first place. If the desire was to improve physician satisfaction, then management should measure it after the plan has been in place for six to twelve months. If the purpose of the plan was to improve the relationship of productivity to compensation for individuals, then the leadership team should measure and report the coefficient of correlation of productivity against compensation. Too many organizations simply measure the effect on the "bottom line" of the finances. Only by communicating the success of the compensation plan in producing the desired effects, however those were defined, will the vitality of the plan be maintained.

COMMUNICATION

The thread of communication runs through all the potential barriers to implementation discussed above. The fact that the compensation system is even being considered for redesign, and the motivation behind that, must be clearly communicated before more sinister motives are attributed. A compelling need for change must be presented to educate the physicians to the current economics of their practice. Physician input must be obtained, with clear expectations created and fulfilled for the redesign and decision-making processes. The model itself must be communicated, but not before it has been tested for accuracy and rationality. Finally, the effects of the plan, and the mechanism for adjustments, must be an ongoing dialogue. Given these multiple and continuous communication needs, it may be wise at the outset to create a formal communication plan, outlining what messages will be communicated at what intervals, to whom, by whom, and by what vehicle.

CONCLUSION

Most compensation models that fail do so just before or after implementation, and usually for one of the reasons discussed in this chapter. The sad irony of that fact is that all of these problems are predictable and solvable at the beginning and throughout the course of compensation system design or redesign. The organization must, however, have an explicit plan to address each issue in an honest fashion; it does not work to have everyone sitting around the table, nodding agreeably to the notion that "We'll just use our usual decision-making process" when that may be flawed, unclear, or non-existent. It is equally unreasonable to agree to grant incentives for visits when the downstream effects of that decision are not considered in detail. The organization that can plan for each of the potential barriers discussed here can create and implement a compensation plan that will work, and thereby demonstrate a model of reasonable design and decision making that may serve the organization well in other arenas.

10

Strategies for Improving Physician Compensation

Kenneth M. Hekman

The bottom line on physician compensation is how to improve the bottom line. In other words, boosting physician compensation requires a combination of individual and group strategies to boost profitability. When individual and group strategies work in harmony, they can achieve extraordinary rewards for the member physicians. When the strategies are in conflict, physician compensation is not the only thing that is compromised; the entire group will suffer from strained relationships, compromises to patient care, and stressful working conditions.

We will explore individual strategies and group strategies in two dimensions. We will look at tactics that both individuals and groups can deploy to work harder and to work smarter. Each tactic in isolation can have a positive impact on the profitability of the practice. When multiple tactics are used in synchronization, the impact can be extraordinary. The strategies are summarized in Table 1.

Think of Table 1 as a menu of options that individuals and groups can choose to boost physician compensation. They can choose the tool that is most comfortable, confident that the impact of coordinated strategies will be positive.

INDIVIDUAL STRATEGIES

Individuals who want to increase their personal income generally can do it through two methods: by working harder or by working smarter. The tactics within these two methods, however, are unlimited.

Table 1 Strategies

	Working Hard	**Working Smart**
Individual	Volume Intensity	Panel Size Patient Management
Group	Capacity Capabilities	Market Position Payer Mix

Working harder means increasing either the volume or the intensity of the physician's efforts. In a fee-for-service environment, volume and intensity are the foundations for reward. The more patients you serve and the greater the risk or invasiveness of the service, the more the physician will get paid. Volume can easily be measured in patient encounters, surgical services or similar measurements. Relative value units (RVUs) are a common measurement for intensity. Increasing intensity comes from learning new procedures and gaining access to the medical technological equipment required to perform those procedures. Increasing volume comes from a variety of tactics. Physicians who want to increase their capacity for patient care should examine their personal time management, consider the number of days and the length of days devoted to patient care, build strong referral relationships, and develop their communication skills to make the most of each patient encounter.

Many physicians feel that they are already working hard enough and are looking for strategies to work smarter instead. Working smarter typically means increasing the panel size (i.e., the number of patients a physician is able to serve) through better patient management techniques. This strategy works particularly well in managed care environments. Patient management techniques are growing, in part due to emerging technologies. Electronic medical records offer physicians capabilities for patient management that are impossible with paper records. Open access scheduling, pioneered by Dr. Mark Murray and Catherine Tantau at Kaiser Permanente, can have a tremendous impact on balancing the supply and demand for physician services. The growth of the Internet is also likely to affect physician capabilities in managing patient care. As practices discover the benefits of enabling patients to schedule their own appointments online, they are opening tremendous potential for improving patient management. Likewise, pioneering groups are exploring how to use e-mail in conjunction with giving patients access to their medical records, especially to help those with chronic medical conditions participate in managing their own care. For example, diabetic patients may benefit greatly from having access to a chart that monitors their glucose levels. Hypertensive patients also may benefit from having access to their physician online for minor pharmaceutical modifications, as well as access to their blood pressure readings over time.

Technological advances such as these require group decisions and group commitments, but individual physicians still must overcome their personal reticence to adopt such strategies in order to benefit from growing panel sizes and improved patient management capabilities.

GROUP STRATEGIES

One of the benefits of being in a medical group is that individual physicians can accomplish more when they function well as a group than any one of them can accomplish on his or her own. Highly profitable groups are those that find strategies that enable the group efforts to be worth more than the sum of its individual parts. While individuals are focusing on their personal efforts at working harder and smarter, group leadership should also be concentrating on their corporate opportunities for enabling everyone to thrive.

Groups can help physicians work harder by examining their capacities and capabilities. If there are barriers to capacity, such as limited exam rooms, limited office hours, limited phone lines and support staff, those capacity decisions will need to be addressed at the group level. Expanding a group's capabilities requires careful planning for adding medical technology or procedural capabilities that are consistent with the group's mission. The initiative for such capability expansions might come from the group or from individual physicians. If a physician is ready to learn a new skill, the management team should support that interest by evaluating the market potential for its success. Administrators likewise can be constantly on the lookout for new procedural capabilities that the market may be looking for, and encourage the group's physicians to consider acquiring the skills necessary to perform them well.

Some groups are exploring their capacities and capabilities by looking beyond the traditional reimbursable services supported by insurance. It's a trend I call "the retailing of medicine." Ophthalmologists have been doing it for years. The optometry business is as much a fashion business as it is a component of healthy eye care. The bulk of eyewear is paid for out-of-pocket, but the proximity of an ophthalmology-owned optical shop makes it a natural choice for patients who already trust the physicians providing their care. The opportunities for expanding medical services in other specialties are beginning to appear in a similar fashion. Primary care physicians are now branching into such cosmetic services as laser hair removal. Nutritional supplements are in demand in some markets and offered by physicians who are ready to support their patients' curiosity about those products. Massage therapy may be a natural adjunct for those involved in orthopedics and physical rehabilitation. Plastic surgery and dermatology are gaining access to a wide variety of cosmetic enhancement therapies, all of which are outside the realm of reimbursable services by insurance companies.

Groups can also think about strategies that enable their physicians to work smarter. Foundational strategies for smart practice include locating the practice in the heart of a market that offers convenient access to the patients that are most likely to need the services, or choosing the insurance contracts that give access to the best employer groups. Another foundational strategy is deliberately determining the payer mix that the group will adopt to balance optimal reimbursement with wise diversity. Market positioning strategies are often overlooked, but they offer excellent potential for enabling individual physicians within the well positioned group to thrive.

Beyond the foundational strategies, groups can also look for ways to help physicians be more efficient in their day-to-day patient care. Groups might make tools available to their member physicians such as training in time management, training in physician-patient communications, patient satisfaction feedback, mentoring or coaching from the most efficient physicians to those who have much to learn, and constant encouragement and support for improving physician efficiency. Technological supports such as electronic medical records and online interactions with patients will most likely require initiation by the group's leadership. Investment planning for such initiatives should take into consideration the impact that efficiency may have on both individual and corporate profitability.

Groups should also constantly monitor their effectiveness at billing and collections efforts, to make sure that the work performed is being paid as well as it can be paid. In that way, administrators and support staff must work smart to support the efficiencies of individual physicians.

CONCLUSION

The strategies for improving physician compensation are unlimited except by the imagination and creativity of well grounded physicians and managers. Designing physician compensation systems is at least as much art as it is science. Physicians need to know themselves, and group leadership needs to understand the organization's market position.

Among all the variations of specialties, geographical settings and market dynamics, one thing emerges as the universal truth. *Trust has to come before compensation systems.* A wise compensation formula may affirm and strengthen foundational trust within a group, but it cannot create trust where there is none. Compensation agreements may be at the core of the complex dynamics that hold a group together, but they are only one of several dynamics. Healthy, sustainable service organizations need to pay attention to all the dynamics, and manage each in a manner that is consistent with all the rest.

I wish to conclude with perspectives from my work with physicians in developing countries. I have had the privilege of advising medical groups in Romania, Honduras and Kyrgyzstan. In developing countries such as these, physicians are often paid government salaries that represent only a fraction of a living wage. In countries where laws are weak and moral fiber has unraveled, physicians find themselves resorting to patient bribery to feed their families. It's a sad commentary on the honorable profession of medicine, and a huge contrast to conditions found in North America.

On the other hand, physician compensation has steadily increased in the United States the last few decades—not for everyone, but for the profession as a whole. According to data from the American Medical Association, physician incomes have typically risen, on average, about 4 percent per year for the last decade. Some specialties have seen advantages greater than others and certainly there are outliers on both ends of the spectrum in every community. But the fact remains that physicians in the United States enjoy incomes that place them in the top 1 percent of the world's population, and with their knowledge and skills, they have the opportunity to enjoy even greater affirmation from the difference they can make in people's lives.

Compensation will always be a poor and inadequate measure of the good that physicians do. So as groups wrestle with the tough decisions about compensation, I hope they never lose sight of the privileges of service. When physicians engage each other with hearts of gratitude for the mysterious and wonderful roles that they play in society, even the daunting challenge of finding an equitable compensation system becomes possible.

Development and Implementation of a New Physician Compensation Plan

JANE PARRISH, FACMPE

This case study was submitted in partial fulfillment of the requirements for election to Fellow status in the American College of Medical Practice Executives (ACMPE).

BACKGROUND

A community hospital developed an affiliated physician group practice. This group was to be the vehicle that would purchase community physician practices and employ physicians. The hospital purchased two practices with a total of ten physicians, seven in group one and three in group two. This was part of the hospital's strategy to maintain market share in their service area. The physician compensation plan included incentive opportunities only for the physicians who had been owners in the purchased practices. All other physicians were compensated with straight salaries. After a year of being employed by the group, the physicians were dissatisfied with the compensation plan.

There were no productivity goals established or communicated to the physician employees at any time during negotiations, or as agreements were signed. Prior to the purchase of these two groups, the hospital, did not communicate any expectations of revenue to be generated. The charge to the senior manager responsible for development of this group was to get the group established by completing the first acquisitions, bringing on board some practices as quickly as possible. The two groups were purchased and agreements signed before the director of practice management was hired. An outside accounting firm performed the practice evaluations. The hospital staff was not familiar with the operations of a community practice or how to measure the productivity of a primary care pediatrician. The physicians did not understand financial statements based on accrual accounting that was provided to them by the hospital.

STATEMENT OF PROBLEM

The problem was two-fold. The productivity of the physicians was lower than expected by the hospital, and the compensation plan was poorly developed. The physicians were disappointed in their salaries, as it soon became evident that their productivity could not support higher salaries. The initial compensation plan had five of the ten physicians compensated with salaries plus incentives. This plan paid incentives based on the productivity of all the physicians in each respective site; productivity was defined by the hospital, not the physicians, and measured by the hospital as cash collections. The physicians receiving incentive payments were original owners of the purchased practices. The plan allowed for a change in base compensation based on productivity; a physician's base salary could increase or decrease based on productivity. Five of the physicians were salaried, with no incentive compensation. These salaried physicians had been working in the practices one year or less at the time of purchase.

Initially the hospital provided to the physicians monthly financial statements based on accrual accounting. The statements were provided at least two months after the close of the month being reported. These statements showed the estimated net revenue and accrued expenses. While the revenue figure was derived from gross charges submitted by the groups, the gross charges, number of visits, number of new patients and cash collections were not recorded. The physicians were accustomed to seeing cash-based financial statements that were provided within one week of the close of the previous month. The groups continued to bill with the practice management systems that were in their offices prior to acquisition, and generated monthly reports that showed gross charges, cash collection and visits totals. However, it became obvious that the physicians no longer received these reports and there were no discussions between the physicians and the hospital regarding the performance of the group. Four months after the acquisitions of the groups, the director of practice operations was hired. At this point timely monthly reports were developed that included gross charges, cash collections and numbers of visits, along with actual expenses incurred during the month. Benchmarks utilizing MGMA standards were utilized to compare the physician's gross charges, visit totals and cash collections.

After one year as employees of the corporation, 67 percent of the physicians from one group experienced a decrease in base salary and received no incentive payments. This plan would have paid incentives based on the total collections of the group to the physicians who had been stockholders of the group prior to purchase. It was noted that one physician would have been paid an incentive if the calculation were based on her productivity alone. If the threshold were divided by the number of eligible physicians, her productivity would have exceeded the threshold by $25,000. This amount was paid to her in quarterly installments to alleviate the effect of the decrease in base salary she experienced. The hospital allowed this to happen in order to retain this young, female, very productive physician. All physicians who were on the straight salary plan maintained their initial salaries.

There was only one physician who was satisfied with the compensation plan in place. He was the original owner of group two. He had received a $50,000 incentive based on the productivity of his site. He received the maximum incentive allowed. The salaried physicians felt that they were subsidizing the physicians receiving incentive compensation. These physicians experienced a 20 percent decrease in salary and were dissatisfied with their lower salaries.

The physicians and the corporation wanted to see compensation and incentives aligned more closely with individual productivity. The hospital directed the group's management to work with the physicians to develop a new compensation plan. The overall productivity was short of the expectations of the hospital, although this fact was not communicated to the physicians. In addition, the hospital saw this situation as an opportunity to address other financial issues of the group. The hospital also had an agenda to reduce the group's expenses and improve the overall financial picture of the group. However, this agenda was not communicated to the physicians as one of the goals of this process. The operational expenses of group one exceeded the MGMA standards for expenses by 51 percent and group two by 46 percent. The hospital wanted to solve all of the problems through increased physician productivity. The hospital decided that a new compensation plan would be the best way to accomplish its goals and that the physicians would accept the new plan if they were included in the development of the plan.

GROUP ONE PRODUCTIVITY

Physician productivity of group one, based on gross charges, decreased 23 percent after purchase. This group's productivity was also well below the 25th percentile levels of the Medical Group Management's Physician Compensation and Productivity Survey,[1] with average charges for pediatric practices which was $294,288 for each individual physician. Two of the physicians' charges were close to the median level of $383,000. The remaining five physicians' productivity was less than the 25th percentile. Only one physician in this group was generating enough revenue to meet her salary, as she consistently saw more patients than her peers. She saw an average of six follow-up visits per hour while her peers saw an average of four follow-up visits per hour.

GROUP TWO PRODUCTIVITY

The senior physician in group two had charges that were just under the 90th percentile of the Medical Group Management's Physician Compensation and Productivity Survey average charges for pediatric practices of $578,986. His base salary of $150,000 was also at the 90th percentile level as measured by the HayGroup best practices compensation salary survey.[2] The junior physician was meeting the 25th percentile for productivity and her salary of $95,000 was at the 25th percentile. The third physician in this group, a specialist, saw patients on a part-time basis and was not included in the incentive plan. This physician was not included in any discussion and his statistics were not included in the data reviewed. The practice's productivity met the levels required to support their base salaries. However, incentive compensation paid to the senior physician was based on productivity of the entire practice.

This data suggested that incentive payments aligned with personal productivity, rather than with the entire site's productivity, would help bring each physician's total compensation more in line with their actual productivity. The hospital hoped a new plan would increase productivity and revenue for the lower producers, and would limit inflated incentive payments to physicians who were not actually producing at a level sufficient to receive bonus payments.

OPTIONS

Options evaluated to address the issues included the following:

1. Continue with all current physician agreements, making no changes to any physician's compensation. This option would not address the physicians' dissatisfaction with the current plan. The physicians would continue to complain of inequities. Incentive payments would continue to be paid to senior physicians based on junior

physician productivity. In addition, the hospital felt that this plan was contributing to the poor financial performance of the groups.

2. Address each physician's compensation plan on an individual basis as the physician raised the issue. The most senior of the new physicians approached the hospital demanding changes to her contract. The senior manager in charge of the groups agreed to make changes to the contract. This contract was not evaluated in the context of the impact that it would have on the financial status of the group as a whole, and it led to other physicians requesting changes to their agreements. While negotiating individual contracts was timely, it was felt that it would not lead to overall physician satisfaction, nor would it lead to improving the financial status of the group.

3. Develop a new compensation plan that would apply to all employed physicians and lead to increased productivity, profit and physician satisfaction. The hospital directed that the group develop a new compensation plan that would be applied to all physicians. The group's senior staff, along with the physicians, would develop this plan. With a new plan for all physicians, the individuals would no longer approach the hospital for new agreements. This approach would give the group's staff the opportunity to evaluate thoroughly the financial impact and to ensure that the plan would improve the financial status of the group. It would also give the physicians input into the development of the plan and therefore gain the participation of all physicians. It was felt that this option would ultimately meet the goals of the hospital: improved physician productivity, improved financial status of the group and improved physician satisfaction.

SOLUTION SELECTED

The hospital's senior management desired that the solution would be to develop a new compensation plan that would more closely align incentives paid to physicians with individual physician productivity. In an effort to decrease the possible confrontational tone of the process, the group's administration decided to utilize a third-party facilitator to guide the process.

THE PROCESS

The facilitator was a physician consultant with experience in developing physician compensation plans. Data were sent to the consultant regarding physician productivity, practice expenses and physician salaries, along with copies of the current incentive plans.

The facilitator met with the group's administration, including the director of finance, the director of practice operations, the director of development who had been involved in initial negotiations with the group and the hospital's senior manager responsible for the group. During this meeting, administration reviewed the group's data as it related to industry standards of physician productivity and physician salaries. The two sources for standards were from MGMA's compensation and productivity survey and HayGroup's best practices compensation survey. The consultant proposed a series of three meetings with a committee of physicians and administrators to review data, suggest and subsequently develop a new plan for the group. The consultant felt that a small committee would be more successful in completing the task in a timely manner. There was to be one meeting to review data, one meeting to discuss options and components of compensation arrangements, and one to finalize a new compensation plan for the group. The entire process was to take one month.

The committee was chosen only by the hospital's senior manager and was to include:

- The group's Director of Practice Operations;
- The group's Director of Finance;
- The Director of Development;
- A physician who had been practicing more than 10 years;
- A physician who had been practicing 1 year;
- A newly recruited physician; and
- The physician consultant as the facilitator.

The physicians were chosen based on the following criteria:

- Representatives from each site;
- Physician representatives with varying levels of practice experience; and
- Physicians with varying expectations from incentive arrangements.

The committee physicians were to represent and inform their peers of all activities of the committee.

The selected members of the committee were notified of scheduled meetings and were sent actual data regarding the practice productivity by physician, salaries by physician, expenses by group, comparable industry standard data, and charts comparing each physician to the industry standards. The data were coded to ensure individual confidentiality.

DATA REVIEW MEETING

During the first meeting, the facilitator introduced the industry standards for physician productivity and compensation from HayGroup and MGMA, compared this to the group's data and outlined the group's problem with the compensation plan. The facilitator also introduced some initial ideas for incentive plans to consider for the development of an incentive plan.

The following charts representing the productivity and salary data were provided for review. The first chart compares each physician's productivity level to the MGMA's productivity report at the 25th percentile for pediatricians. The 25th percentile data was chosen for the benchmark, as most of the physicians' productivity levels were lower than this benchmark, which was the lowest available in the MGMA survey.

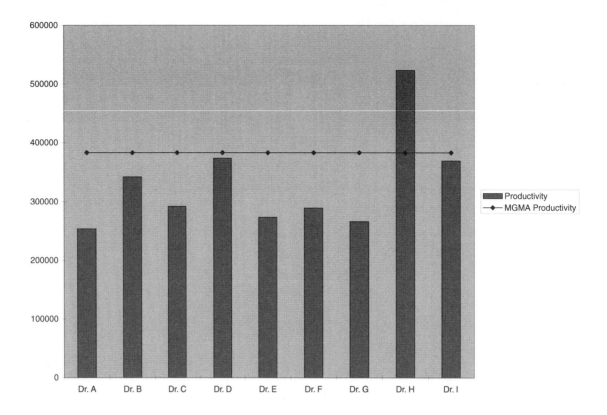

The following chart represents the salaries as compared to the 25th percentile salaries for pediatricians from the HayGroup.

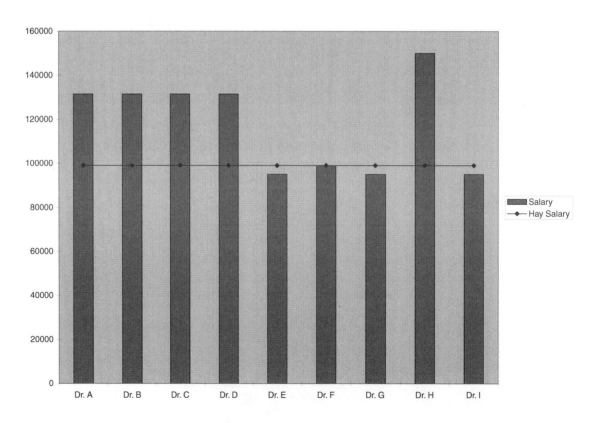

The physicians had no comments regarding the information presented during this initial meeting. The physicians' main concern was that all of the group's physicians were not part of the committee. After many discussions outside of the committee, the hospital's senior manager agreed to allow all the employed physicians to participate in the meetings. The first meeting was repeated with all physicians in attendance. While the physicians were not pleased with the data, they were unable to dispute it, as each individual group generated their own raw data.

There were additional meetings to discuss various components of a compensation plan. The committee agreed that the basic components of the plan would include a base salary equal to the 25th percentile ($99,000) of the HayGroup's best practices survey, and an opportunity for incentives based on productivity in excess of a threshold. The threshold was $294,000 for the first year. There were also gainsharing opportunities if expenses were managed below budgets.

Many of the discussions were controversial and contentious, creating bad feelings toward the hospital and among the physicians themselves. In trying to protect their individual incomes, some of the physicians made comments that were harmful to their peers. The younger physicians pointed out that the older physicians had decreased their productivity but continued to have higher salaries than the younger physicians who were the higher producers. The physicians who did not benefit from the practice purchase price made statements to the effect that these physicians had received their money and were now not willing to work hard enough to make the practice successful.

Initially the consultant stated that it would take three to four meetings over the course of one month to develop a new compensation plan. It actually took five months and numerous meetings to develop and present the plan to the group's board of directors. Formal meetings were scheduled and held with all physicians, the group's administration and the facilitator. The plan was implemented immediately following the board's approval.

THE PLAN

The incentive plan developed by the group included a base salary of $99,000 for all physicians. Each physician had the opportunity to receive incentive compensation based on individual productivity after his or her productivity reached $294,000 of gross charges. The physician would receive 32 percent of all gross charges over the threshold. The physician contributed 10 percent of his or her incentive toward a group bonus. The base salary and incentive thresholds were prorated based on part-time and medical leave time.

In addition, there was a group incentive based on overall productivity of the group. Each group was allowed to decide the distribution of its group incentive. The groups decided to give administrative credits for academic and administrative tasks. The groups' administrative personnel did not participate in the group incentive decisions and did not know the method used to determine how this bonus would be distributed.

While it was recognized that the thresholds should be measured by cash collections, the hospital agreed to base the thresholds on charges discounted for historical collection rates. This concession was made by the hospital because there was a new billing system in place, and the cash collections had decreased with the conversion to a new system. However, the plan was to move toward using cash collections as the measurement in one year. The plan also called for development of an additional bonus based on budget management. If a group was able to manage its operational expenses (all expenses less physician salaries, bonuses, and benefits), the group would receive an additional bonus to be distributed within the group. For example, in year one if group one spent only 95 percent of its budget, then 30 percent of the savings would be allocated into the physician gainsharing pool. (This portion of the plan was not implemented, as the group was dissolved prior to the completion of the budgeting process.) In an effort to decrease the impact of decreased base salaries for some physicians, incentives were to be calculated and paid quarterly with a yearly reconciliation.

RESULTS

The compensation committee did negotiate a new incentive compensation plan. However, the relationships between the hospital and the physicians were damaged. The physicians saw this process as a way for the hospital to make them work harder and receive less compensation. The confusing goals and agendas of the process created a lack of trust between the physicians and the hospital. The relationships among the physicians were also damaged, as each physician tried to protect his own income. Statements were made that created bad feelings among the physicians. There were conflicting and confusing goals associated with this process. The hospital stated that the goal for the plan was to increase physician satisfaction, improve productivity and better align incentive payments with individual productivity. The physicians each came to the table with an individual goal of increasing his or her own compensation. The hospital also had the unstated goal of improving the overall financial status of the group.

The original goal for the new compensation plan was to better align physician compensation with individual productivity. Initial calculations for the incentive payments were completed, resulting in an overall net increase of salaries paid to physicians, but there was not a substantial increase in overall productivity. At the time of the first quarterly calculation of incentive payments, eight of the ten physicians received incentive payments. Two of the physicians would experience a further decrease in base salary if their productivity did not increase throughout the balance of the year.

All physicians in the group had agreed to the new compensation plan, except for one senior physician who refused to accept the new plan. His contract stated that his compensation would be based on the productivity of the entire practice, and there was one year left on the agreement. This physician was the most productive of all the physicians in the group, and he had worked hard to transition his practice to a younger physician. In addition, the site was located in an underserved area. The losses of approximately $350,000 shown in this practice were recognized by the hospital as furthering its charitable mission to their service area. The only alternative for the hospital would have been to default on this contract. Therefore, the hospital felt there was no choice but to honor this contract. He continued to be paid based on his site's productivity. The new incentive plan also allowed the second physician in that practice to be paid an incentive, resulting in a net increase of salaries for this group.

One group had two physicians who did not perform to the minimum level. Incentives were paid to the remaining physicians based on individual productivity. Even with incentive payments, four physicians experienced further decreases in overall compensation with the new plan. The physicians who had been owners of the group before acquisition had experienced a steady decrease in salary since acquisition.

The process to negotiate a new compensation plan, the hidden agendas of the parties and arguments proved to damage relationships between the hospital and the physicians of group one beyond repair. The relationship was tenuous before this process began. The physicians had sold their practices to a respected hospital and had been promised that they would be part of a large network of community practices and would receive improved managed care contracts, improved purchasing power, marketing and advertisement of their practices. The hospital had changed its strategy after purchasing just two practices and did not grow the large network. The physicians were seeing none of the promised benefits of selling their practices. Negotiations began to sever group one from the hospital after the first quarter's incentive calculation.

LESSONS LEARNED

1. Compensation issues are individual and personal. While a small committee can accomplish more, one must trust the committee members implicitly to represent individual needs. In this situation, the physicians did not trust the hospital. Further, the physicians were not comfortable that their peers who were initially selected for the committee would represent all of the individual needs.

2. The hospital purchased community-based, primary care practices without developing productivity goals that would need to be met in order for the group to be successful. They did not communicate to the physicians an expected level of productivity or an expected financial outcome of the arrangement.

3. The hospital needed to complete more comprehensive financial reviews of the plan. Productivity data showed that low performers would not support even the reduced salaries.

4. The plan was developed with the understanding that all physicians would participate or the plan would not be implemented. However the hospital ultimately allowed one physician to opt out of the plan. This exception increased the overall physician compensation, and thus expenses, in this site. This decision contributed to the overall financial failure of the plan.

5. The hospital recognized that change is achieved more easily when all parties are involved in the examination of the data and planning of new procedures. However, the hospital allowed only token involvement by the physicians in developing a new incentive plan, selecting a facilitator and committee participants. The hospital should have involved the physicians and office managers in evaluating the entire financial situation and worked toward solutions together.

6. The facilitator was chosen because he was a physician. The hospital paid for the title of "physician" so that it would appear that a person with a solid understanding of the needs of physicians would be managing the process. The hospital expected the physician facilitator to improve the physician buy-in to the process. The facilitator was not able to manage the discussions of the group and did not manage the process in the manner in which it was described to the hospital's staff.

The group was to have been a 75 physician group by the time this process took place. There were ten physicians and no plans to grow the group. The physicians were not seeing the benefits of joining this practice, that is, improved managed care contracting, decreased expenses, decreased administrative tasks, marketing and name recognition of being associated with this hospital. This process served to further destroy relationships with these physicians, and was the issue that finally led to the dissolution of the group. It was obvious that the hospital was not going to grow this practice and had in fact moved on to a different strategy to gain market share. It would have been easier and less adversarial to begin discussions to dissolve the group much earlier in the process.

BIBLIOGRAPHY

1. *Physician Compensation and Production Survey: 1999 Report Based on 1998 Data.* Englewood, CO: Medical Group Management Association; 1999. p 78, 79.

2. *Best Practices Survey,* excerpts. Jersey City, NJ: Hay Research For Management; 1999

Transitioning Employed Physicians from Fixed Salaries to Production-Based Compensation in a Large, Hospital-Affiliated Multi-Specialty Group Practice

JAMES R. WURTS, FACMPE

This case study was submitted in partial fulfillment of the requirements for election to Fellow status in the American College of Medical Practice Executives.

STATEMENT OF PROBLEM

A large multispecialty group, affiliated with a not-for-profit health system, was faced with the challenge of transitioning its members from fixed salaries into a production-based methodology of compensation. These compensation discussions occurred during a time when issues relating to both retention of physicians and the group's future were in some question. The ultimate compensation product had to be fair, easy to administer, motivational in nature, and compliant with applicable legal and regulatory requirements.

ADMINISTRATIVE DATA

Local Economy and Market

The community in which the group practice is located is found in the heart of the Southwest and is a major regional center for business and industry. The city's population is over 200,000 people, and its age distribution is somewhat younger than the national norm. Future population growth is expected to be steady, but not rapid, with only minor population increases projected within the next 10 years. The median family income level is comparable to the rest of the U.S. The city serves as the major retail trade center and health care provider for a large multi-state geographic area comprised of more than 1.5 million people. The health care sector of the community employs approximately 11,000 people, nearly 1/10 of the local employed workforce, and its payroll and related contributions provide an impact of more than $500,000,000 to the area's economy. There are 66 clinics and 700 physicians in the city.

There are three major hospitals, a church-affiliated facility of 400 beds, a private not-for-profit facility of 600 beds, and a medium-sized teaching hospital affiliated with a local medical school. The local medical community enjoys a wide drawing area and an excellent reputation as a tertiary referral center. There is a large concentration of primary care physicians and specialists in the community. Traditionally, physicians have enjoyed income levels higher than national norms.

Changing Market Conditions

In the mid-1990s, many local physicians began to notice changes in their practices, as patients were transitioning into managed care plans from the traditional commercial plans based on payment of full fees. Also, many local physicians were experiencing changes in their practices related to the Medicare program. There were no capitation products in the market. By this time, various market forces led the hospital systems to consider the employment of physicians in hospital-affiliated group practice models. This strategy was felt to be justified on the basis of offering managed care plans single signature contracting, to provide preparation for the assumption of risk and, most importantly, to further align physicians with their employing health care system.

The Group

In response to these market conditions, the private hospital system determined it was in its strategic interest to develop a multispecialty group closely aligned to its goals. The group was organized under a private foundation model necessitated by the fact that the State had in place a prohibition against the corporate practice of medicine. The foundation model was utilized as a vehicle by which non-profit facilities could employ physicians through the establishment of a corporation, solely governed by physicians, but with ties to a corporate "Member" with certain reserved powers, largely financial. The group eventually employed almost 100 physicians, with the distribution being 60 percent primary care and 40 percent specialists.

A non-physician chief administrative officer was hired, as were several practice managers and an MSO director with responsibility for billing and accountancy functions. The board of directors of the company included seven physicians, all members of the group (referred to hereafter as the Group).

The model employed in assembling the Group involved purchase of practice assets of established local physicians, including accounts receivable, office equipment, buildings and goodwill. The Group assumed any property leases held by the physicians. The physicians who became employees of the Group worked for a fixed monthly salary and were provided a reasonable fringe benefit package. The Group took all responsibility for billing, collections, employment of support personnel, procurement of supplies and equipment, establishment of fee schedules, managed care contracting and all other practice support. In addition to the practices, the Group operated some ancillary services, including a full-service clinical laboratory, limited radiology facilities, and a physical therapy clinic. The 100 practices in the Group were in 30 different locations, ranging in size from a 25-physician multispecialty internal medicine group all the way to several solo practices.

Other Issues within the Group

Initially, the Group's operations were fraught with problems. Assessment of the Group's difficulties revealed several problems, including lack of meaningful physician incentives within the Group's compensation structure, thus limiting opportunities to influence production and control costs on the part of the physicians. It was felt the development of an incentive plan that would reward appropriate behaviors and discourage negative behaviors would be essential to the Group's development.

COMPENSATION METHODOLOGIES

All the members of the Group were paid a flat salary, which approximated recent earnings prior to entering the Group. The initial employment contracts were externally determined to be fair market value and contained no standards for production. Knowledgeable attorneys were utilized to assure that all applicable legal requirements were met. All fees generated and collected belonged to the Group. All patient records belonged to the Group, as well. Due to contract restrictions, the Group had no ability to move the physicians or consolidate them into more effective practice arrangements. The Group provided professional liability insurance and a paid fringe benefit program that approximated industry standards.

Most of the contracts were for an initial term of five years' duration. There was a provision in the agreement for termination for cause.

The initial contracts had a non-compete clause, which prohibited the physician from engaging in competitive activities during the duration of the contract and one year thereafter. Also, the physician could not engage in outside activities without express permission from the Group.

The contract included a provision giving the Group the ability to pay an annual bonus related to such matters as cooperation, adherence to utilization review guidelines, favorable quality assurance results, contribution to the reduction of overhead and expenses, attitude, favorable interpersonal relationships and related subjective guidelines. The payment of this bonus was not mandatory, but subject to the overall financial performance of the Group.

ALTERNATIVES CONSIDERED

In going forward, it was determined that the Group had essentially four options concerning transforming physician compensation methodologies. These options included:

1. Keep the present contracts intact.
2. Develop bonus arrangements based upon the profitability of the practice.
3. Develop productivity incentives as measured by gross charges.
4. Develop a compensation system based upon a mixture of behavioral and production incentives.

SELECTION OF ALTERNATIVES

More History

The Group had an opportunity to exercise a "trial and error" approach in the selection of compensation alternatives over the five-year life of the initial agreements. As new physicians entered the Group, different compensation methodologies were employed. In effect, the use of these methodologies gave the Group an opportunity to test compensation methods on a small group of doctors, with limited downside risk. All of these methods were reviewed by outside consultants to determine that compensation was at fair market value.

The Group's financial situation kept the option of keeping the contracts intact from being seriously considered.

Profit Sharing

The first methodology of bonus payments based on profit was offered to approximately six physicians who entered the Group in 1996. The basic terms of these contracts allowed the physician to participate in an incentive program that, over and above a determined base salary, divided equally between the Group and the physician. Annual profit was defined as the amount of money remaining from professional fees generated and collected after all overhead expenses were deducted. This so-called profit was divided between the physician and the Group with the norm being a split of 75 percent to the physician and 25 percent to the Group.

This particular contract form proved to be unsatisfactory to all parties. The physicians complained that their income was adversely affected by the Group's inability to collect from patients and insurers effectively, the tendency of the Group to charge-off high amounts to bad debt and contractual allowances, poorly thought-out managed care contracting decisions, and the insistence that, in fulfillment of the parent organization's non-profit mission, care be provided to indigents and Medicaid recipients. Also, the physicians under this arrangement complained that the Group's overhead was excessively high. In all cases, there were virulent disagreements between the physicians and the Group Administrators regarding calculations of bonuses. For all six physicians, these contracts were renegotiated to fixed base salary agreements.

Gross Charge Based Bonuses

After the profit-based methodology failed, contracts were offered to three new physicians, providing a base salary and an incentive plan giving a physician the opportunity to earn additional compensation based upon the annual productivity performance of the physician's individual practice. The award amount was determined as a multiple of base salary to net revenues. Under this plan, if a physician's level of gross charges exceeded the base salary by a certain multiple, he or she would receive a monetary bonus at the end of the year. For example, if the revenue target were $450,000, which equaled three times base salary, the physician would be eligible for a bonus payment of $50,000.

These agreements also proved problematic, since the revenue targets ended up being essentially unattainable, especially for entry-level physicians. Providing physicians with an unrealistic bonus target proved very destructive, and these plans were also transitioned out.

The Initial Experiment with Combined Production and Behavioral Incentives

The next compensation methodology tested by the Group involved a combination of productivity and behavioral incentives. The physician received a base salary. Over and above the base salary, the physician was given the opportunity to earn incentive compensation. The incentive opportunity involved a mixture of production and behavioral incentives, which allowed for the generation of additional income. Also, the incentive plan was written with the flexibility of allowing transition to other plans. This flexibility was of particular concern, since if capitated care entered the market, the Group needed the ability to shift the incentives away from pure production to effective medical management in a risk assumption environment.

The incentive program involved a mixture of patient satisfaction determinants, as measured by scores on the Group's standard patient evaluation survey; productivity, as measured by ambulatory encounters and Resource Based Relative Value Units, and quality, based upon a chart audit-based peer review program, developed by the Group's Quality Management Committee. If the physician received maximum scores in all parameters, his or her compensation could be increased. The weightings of the measures with regard to the bonus were 60 percent productivity, 20 percent patient satisfaction, and 20 percent quality review. Also within this system, if maximum standards were achieved, the Group could establish the physician at a higher base salary for subsequent contract years.

This program ended up having very mixed results. Many of the physicians achieved higher levels of productivity under this system, especially those in procedurally oriented practices. It appeared more difficult, however, for primary care physicians to achieve levels of productivity needed to trigger the bonus system. Almost all of the physicians received maximum scores on the patient satisfaction and quality measures. There was some concern that the standards in this area were too low. The biggest problem with this particular system was the fact that it required excessive staff time to administer the quality assurance reviews and compile reports to the physicians relating to RVUs and ambulatory encounters. Explaining to the physicians their progress in meeting the standards took excessive clerical and administrative support during a period of time when the Group was, in fact, downsizing the support staff to meet financial goals mandated by the parent organization. Also, it was discovered that many physicians did not understand the RVU system. The final verdict was that if the Group had a greater level of maturity and if better quality and patient management systems in place, this system may have indeed worked well, but at the Group's immature stage of development, a far simpler plan was needed.

It became clear at this juncture that while the production/behavioral compensation methodology was essentially sound, a plan that was simple to administer and easy to understand was needed to both retain membership and drive greater revenue.

PROCEDURES TO SELECT SOLUTION

Shaping a Compensation Project

Requests for proposals were sent to three nationally recognized consulting firms asking for assistance in the finalization of a broad-based physician incentive plan for the Group. The process of selecting the consultants involved evaluation of our needs, interviews with principals from the firms and a reference check involving telephone interviews with recent clients. The selection process involved both the Group administrator and selected physicians. Interestingly enough, the pricing for this engagement was very similar from all three firms. After the onsite interviews and reference checks, the decision was made by the Group board to select one of the nationally recognized firms to assist with the process. Also at this point, an adhoc compensation committee was selected to work with the board in the actual implementation and design of the system. This committee included the group administrator and four physicians representing the key specialty areas in the Group. Also the group's legal counsel was utilized extensively to assure any proposed compensation plan complied with all applicable legal requirements, particularly the Stark regulations.

Incidentally, the consultant's role in the process turned out to be minimal. Only minor "fine-tuning" was required in the basic plan arrived at by the Group through the above-described "trial and error" methods.

In the interests of validating the group's experiences and conclusions concerning compensation, a survey was conducted of the physician members of the Group concerning compensation and behavioral expectations. The Group achieved an 8 percent return rate and found the greatest physician concerns were with the fairness and equity of the system. After several meetings stretching out over a six-month period, a model compensation program was brought forward to the members of the Group. The Group's board of directors was also heavily involved in this process, hearing several presentations on the various models, and making the ultimate selection decision.

The Final Model

The final compensation model involved offering each physician a base salary that reflected the physicians' production as benchmarked by national standards. The methodology used in this process took the physicians' charges for personally performed services (ancillary and nonphysician providers services omitted), and benchmarked these charges against the norms for his specialty as expressed in the *Physician Compensation and Production Survey* of Medical Group Management Association. After production was expressed in terms of a percentile, this percentile was indexed to the MGMA's compensation parameters. A physician for a particular specialty section performing in the 75th percentile for production would be compensated at the 75th percentile for compensation, geographically adjusted. In each case, an opinion letter was obtained from an outside compensation consultant to validate the determination and also provide protection to both the physician and the Group in case an inference was made of excessive compensation.

In addition to the base compensation policy, the Group adopted a physician productivity standard that stated its physicians must achieve and maintain productivity levels consistent with the levels used to determine their compensation at fair market value. In the event the physician exceeded the productivity standards in their base contract for a 12-month period by 10 percent or greater, the Group had the ability to adjust base compensation upward. Conversely, if production dropped more than 10 percent, a downward adjustment in compensation could take place. If production dropped 20 percent or more, the Group had the ability to unilaterally terminate the physician's contract. A provision was built into the policy which provided that, if the drop took place for extenuating circumstances, the Group could waive salary reduction or termination. In this case, extenuating circumstances were defined as illness, disability, certain actions of third parties, including managed care entities, and the like.

In addition to the base salary, the Group had the ability to grant a physician a 10 percent discretionary annual bonus. This bonus would be based on a performance evaluation conducted annually by the chief medical officer in consultation with the Group administrator and Section Medical Directors. The process would compare the physician's performance status in comparison to peers within the Group, as well as to recognized regional and national standards. Tools used to evaluate performance would include patient satisfaction surveys, quality improvement documents, incident reports, productivity reports and personal observations. A decision was made to do the annual review in August of each year under a "forced ranking" system which compared performance of Group members. Among the parameters specifically utilized in the review were participation in community benefit activities, performance as a compatible member of the Group, general attitude, and personal relations, participation in Group meetings and activities, efforts to support cost-effective care, reports of dysfunctional behavior, patient satisfaction survey results, medical practice accessibility and productivity, being actively available to see patients in a non-discriminatory manner, acceptance of new patients, size of primary care panels, total gross charges, quality of records, adherence to utilization review policies, and so on. It was anticipated that this review would be conducted through the issuance of a "report card," demonstrating certain statistical parameters for the physician, as well as obtaining subjective reports from medical directors and others aware of the physician's performance.

Achieving Physician Buy-In

In an effort to achieve buy-in to the new compensation program, presentations were made, not only to the board of directors, but to the section medical director and to the Group's general membership. Presentations took place in the form of a series of small group meetings with the administrator, chief medical officer and the Group attorney being present. In addition, a new contract embracing these changes was sent to each Group member for a "public comment" period, in which the physicians had an opportunity to actually review the contract language, consult with their attorneys and offer changes and suggestions. Several suggestions were incorporated into the final contract document.

FINAL DECISION

After several periods of trial and error, the Group adopted the contract format outlined above. It is interesting to note that in the year this contract format was adopted, productivity, measured by gross charges adjusted for increases in fee schedules, increased 14.5 percent. The Group's bottom line performance improved significantly. The introduction of the new contracts occurred coincidental with the expiration of the initial Group employment agreements. Use of the new contract format, and netting out retirements and other planned exits, the Group enjoyed a retention rate of 80 percent. As their compensation plans were being altered, exit options were developed for physicians who wished to return to private practice in a manner that preserved relationships with the parent health system.

LESSONS LEARNED

Performance management in groups is inherently linked to compensation. When individuals perform effectively for an organization, they expect to be compensated fairly for their efforts. Physicians are no different in this sense from other individuals working in large organizations. They want to be recognized for the work they do. While there are many intrinsic rewards to practicing medicines, physicians want to feel they have been paid fairly for the work they accomplish. The operative word here is "fairly." The overall test of any compensation system is its equity and alignment of physician incentives with achievement of the overall goals of the organization.

The key lesson learned in this case was that a compensation plan for a large group practice must support the parent organization's values and strategies, while respecting economic realities. The system must provide the group with the ability to attract, motivate and retain superior physicians by balancing market competitiveness and fiscal responsibility. The selected compensation system appeared to achieve these goals, particularly as evidenced by productivity and profitability increases achieved after its inception, as well as retention performance. The use of a system based on gross charges was especially important for this group in that it removed from the physician any reluctance to see indigent or Medicaid patients. This factor was of great importance to the parent organization. By taking down these barriers, the system helped the physicians achieve an even greater value to the religiously sponsored non-profit parent organization.

Obviously a compensation system should be legal. The Group took extreme care to use consultants and knowledgeable attorneys to validate the fair market nature of its compensation packages, and removed ancillaries from the compensation determination, thus avoiding Stark law issues.

Compensation systems must be simple, understandable, and easy to administer. Our gross-charge-based formula was a model of simplicity, very easy to explain to physicians and equally easy to monitor a physician's progress throughout the year. The Group had failed miserably using RVUs, ambulatory encounters, multiple behavioral determinants, and so on. Additionally, the system took only a minimal amount of time, largely on the part of the Group administrator, to explain and communicate to the physicians.

The Group also learned a lesson that a plan should be flexible. Its market was largely discounted fee-for-service, with no capitation whatsoever. The Group saw many consultants, with limited market knowledge, try to inflict a more complicated plan based on "at-risk" managed care determinants. The authors of a compensation plan should have a full understanding of the payor market and shape the plan accordingly. At the same time, the plan should be flexible and help manage the transition from fee-for-service, should capitation occur. The plan, by including some rudimentary quality and patient satisfaction parameters in the subjective bonus system, would ultimately allow for this transition.

A compensation plan should be driven by data. The quality of the data was very important. Frankly, in the early days of the Group, problems with multiple data sets, very primitive MIS systems, and inconsistency of fee schedules made it very difficult to produce consistently credible numbers. By the time the compensation plan was finalized, these problems had been remedied. Physicians actually began to trust the data generated by the Group's Finance Department. The plan included a vehicle to report on a regular basis to Group members their progress throughout the year, giving physicians the ability to improve production. Also, it was felt with this regular monitoring, there would be no untoward surprises for the physician at bonus or renegotiation times.

A plan should feature goals that are attainable. It only frustrates physicians when goals are too lofty for mortals to achieve. A physician could attain the performance goals set forth in our plan. Actually, at the end of the most recent year, it was found that the majority of our physicians were performing at the MGMA 75th percentile or above. Also, the typical bonus paid under the subjective bonus plan was 8 percent. The fact that several of our physicians who had entered into new contracts under the compensation plan attained bonuses early on, helped sell other Group members on both the plan and the credibility of management. It was very important that this process be thoroughly integrated with the performance evaluation system.

Most importantly, a successful compensation plan must be meaningful to both the organization and to the participants from a financial and behavioral viewpoint. There must be some certainty that if certain behaviors take place bonuses will be paid. In addition, a plan must include mechanisms to increase the potential for additional compensation from year-to-year for those physicians who exceed established goals. The Group's inclusion of an ability to raise base salary "raised the bar" for high achievers and drove increased production.

While performance management is a common procedure for most organizational employees, it tends to be an uncommon procedure for physicians in group practices. Doing performance evaluations on a group of nearly 100 physicians proved a challenge for the parties on both ends of the review process. However, group leadership became convinced that this process, along with its integration with the mission and values of the organization, ultimately produced a stronger group with even closer alignment to the parent organization.

A New Paradigm in Academic Health Centers
Productivity-Based Physician Compensation

Margie C. Andreae, MD, and Gary L. Freed, MD, MPH

Now more than ever, health care organizations with employed physicians are focusing on their compensation arrangements. The Balanced Budget Act of 1997 and recent changes in managed care contracts have resulted in declining reimbursement for professional services, with no indication of a reversal in the trend. With fewer dollars at hand, organizations are taking a closer look at their most costly expenditures—physician salaries and fringe benefits.

Three Ways to Lower Physician Compensation

Health care organizations may reduce the cost of physician compensation in a number of ways. One is to reduce the size of the physician work force through layoffs or attrition. Another is to freeze or reduce physician compensation. A third is to redesign the compensation program, linking physician pay to productivity.

All three of these approaches can lower compensation costs, but each has a different impact on the organization. Decreasing the size of the physician work force can cut losses quickly but most likely will result in the provision of fewer services and fewer revenue-generating opportunities. Reducing physicians' salaries deflates morale and increases turnover. Redesigning compensation plans is the strategy with the greatest potential to cut costs while maintaining services and enhancing physician productivity.

Performance-based compensation or incentive plans are not new to most health care organizations. According to a 1994 physician compensation survey of hospitals, integrated health systems, physician group practices and HMOs, sponsored by the American Hospital Association, the Healthcare Financial Management Association, the American Society for Healthcare Human Resources Administration and Ernst & Young LLP, 56 percent awarded bonuses or incentive pay to their physician employees.[44] However, despite the wide use of incentive plans, the literature lacks descriptions of individual programs, making it difficult to identify why some may work better than others.

Instead, articles about incentive plans tend to offer survey results or other generalized conclusions. For example, the 1994 physician compensation survey found that incentive pay usually composed only 5 percent to 15 percent of total compensation and was often based on subjective measures resulting in little overall impact on physician productivity.[45]

A 1999 Towers Perrin study of physician compensation concluded that hospital-owned primary care networks tend to lose money because their cash-compensation plans fail to align physician incentives with those of the larger health care system.[46] While these studies provide valuable points of consideration, they have limited usefulness in designing or evaluating an individual program.

When we undertook the challenge of designing a compensation program for a large group of academic general pediatricians in the Division of General Pediatrics at the University of Michigan Health System, we found the literature devoid of descriptive accounts to aid us in our task. Here we give a detailed description of our program and a review of key elements in its formulation, to assist others as they struggle with this challenge.

PROGRAM DESIGN

We developed an innovative productivity-based compensation program for primary care pediatricians at the University of Michigan that aligns with the goals of the health system, which are to:

- Improve clinical outcomes and service;
- Support the health science academic teaching mission;
- Enhance financial strength and competitiveness;
- Improve patient satisfaction; and
- Create and apply new knowledge in health care.

We based our program on the premise that productivity will increase if physicians have an incentive to produce more than the minimum.[47] Unlike traditional academic compensation models, our program financially rewards physicians for clinical productivity that exceeds minimum standards.

We designed the program for a division of 35 academic general pediatricians. These faculty are part of a primary care network comprising 12 single-specialty and multispecialty ambulatory care centers. Each physician has an active role in both patient care and education of residents and medical students. Some have research and/or administrative responsibilities.

We designed the program goals for the faculty to be specific, measurable and attainable. This was important to achieve faculty buy-in and maintain morale and a healthy, competitive work environment. The plan rewards faculty fairly for their efforts in patient care, education and research, while at the same time giving them autonomy and responsibility for their own productivity. Faculty receive a financial incentive to be creative and proactive in areas of clinical practice management where they previously believed they had no control and often maintained little interest (Table 1).

PERFORMANCE MEASUREMENTS

Our program measures performance in three different areas—clinical performance, education and research—with the greatest emphasis on clinical performance. In seeking to determine a clinical performance outcome that we could monitor easily and accurately, we evaluated the advantages and disadvantages of several measures of clinical productivity

Table 1   Practice Management Areas Where Physician Input
Can Enhance Productivity

- Marketing
- Work area redesign
- Schedule templates
- Hours of operation
- Services provided
- Role of support staff
- "Late" and "no show" policy

(Table 2). Of these, we chose the work component of the relative value unit (RVU) of the resource-based relative value system (RBRVS).[48] In the RBRVS, a work RVU is linked to every Current Procedural Terminology (CPT) code. Services that require more effort are assigned a higher work RVU. Compared with gross charges, collections or visit numbers, the work RVU is standardized for the type and complexity of each visit and most closely reflects the physician's clinical work effort. Importantly, with an RVU-based program, physicians are not held at risk for payor mix or the reimbursement structure of managed care contracts for which they have little input in our health system.

Selection of the work RVU as our clinical performance measure allowed us to align physician performance with the health system's goal of increasing patient access, while not discouraging the management of complex cases. A physician can generate more RVUs by increasing patient visit numbers and/or providing care to patients with complex medical problems.

After choosing the RVU as our performance measure, we defined a standard or benchmark to make the application of the clinical productivity measurement meaningful to both the faculty and the health system. For credibility among faculty as well as institutional support, the standards must rest on sound data. We used the Medical Group Management Association (MGMA) Physician Compensation and Production Survey Report because it has one of the highest respondent rates for general pediatrics.[49] This report covers average work RVU production and compensation per RVU for a wide range of specialties. We used the median work RVU for a general pediatrician as the benchmark for clinical productivity in our program.

Table 2   Quantitative Clinical Performance Measures

Measure	Advantages	Disadvantages
Gross charges	Easy to measure	Dependent on fee schedule
Collections	Direct link to cash flow	Varies with insurance contracts
Patient visits	Easy to measure	Discourages management of complex cases; not linked to cash flow
Patient contact hours	Easy to measure	Does not measure work effort; not linked to cash flow
Relative value units	Standardized measure of work effort	Not linked to cash flow

We measured education of trainees as a performance area. Teaching is a core mission of academic health systems, yet the dollars to support this activity are dwindling. Many fear that too much emphasis on clinical productivity will persuade physicians to decrease or even abandon teaching duties.[50] We developed a teaching credit to offset estimated losses in clinical productivity while precepting, based on the assumption that medical students have a net negative impact on clinical productivity. As a performance measure, we chose to use hours spent with medical students in patient care settings.

In contrast, educating residents in continuity clinic does not decrease the productivity of attending faculty when averaged over a resident's three years.[51] Our program, which employs both a one-on-one arrangement and the traditional staff model for precepting in the continuity clinics, credits faculty with the work RVUs generated by any resident-staffed patient encounter.

The majority of faculty in our division work on a clinical track; a few focus on research. For those receiving extramural salary support for research, we apply the percentage of time funded as the measure for this effort.

COMPONENTS OF THE PROGRAM

The total physician salary has five components:

1. Base;

2. Clinical incentive;

3. Academic supplement ;

4. Administrative differential; and

5. Teaching credit.

Base Salary Component

The base salary is defined not as a percentage of the total salary but as a percentage of our RVU productivity benchmark. We set our base at 70 percent of the benchmark RVUs with the expectation that every faculty member should be able to meet this level of productivity to cover the cost of his/her base salary. We term this expectation "minimum RVU requirement to cover base," and it should not be confused with benchmark RVUs—the productivity standard or target set for an individual's overall clinical performance. The base is converted into a monetary figure using the median compensation per RVU ($/RVU) for a general pediatrician as reported in the latest annual MGMA survey.

All faculty members, regardless of rank, receive the same base salary, but total salary will vary depending on annual performance. In our university system, the base component is guaranteed annually. By requiring faculty to earn their base salary first, we decrease the financial risk placed on the health system. Consequences of not earning the base component are described below. After meeting the minimum RVU requirement to cover base, faculty members become eligible for the clinical incentive component.

Clinical Incentive Component

The clinical incentive component is analogous to a bonus paid for any RVUs generated in excess of the minimum required to cover the base salary. We use the same $/RVU formula to convert this measurement into an incentive payment. By using the same $/RVU, we reward faculty at a fair market rate for extending hours, adding patients to their schedules and maximizing their coding accuracy, especially for complex cases. We expect experienced clinicians to be more skilled at time and practice management issues, earning a higher salary as a result. The total salary cap is set at the MGMA 90th percentile for a general pediatrician. All faculty have the opportunity to augment their incomes by extending hours or enhancing efficiencies.

Academic Supplement Component

Individuals with a significant amount of grant-funded salary support can earn an academic supplement. The grant-funded salary amount is transferred from base salary to the supplement. The dollar amount is converted into RVUs using the $/RVU formula. The minimum RVU requirement to cover base salary is then reduced by this amount, eliminating a clinical productivity requirement for this portion of salary. When an individual's grant funding expires, that portion of his/her salary reverts back to a clinically supported base.

Administrative Differential Component

We add an administrative differential to the salaries of faculty with an administrative appointment paid by the service appointing them. Administrative service positions in our system include health center medical directors, medical education directors and service chiefs. In addition to the administrative differential, the minimum RVUs required to cover the base salary are reduced by the percentage of effort assigned to this activity. The individual still receives his/her full base salary, but the clinical productivity requirement for this administrative portion is eliminated.

Teaching Credit Component

As noted above, we developed a teaching credit in the form of an annual salary supplement. It replaces anticipated clinical productivity lost by precepting a medical student on a required clinical service. A University of Michigan Medical School task force estimated that faculty experience a 20 percent decrease in productivity while working with medical students.[52] Based on this estimate, we converted hours spent with students into work RVU credits as shown in Table 3.

Table 3 Calculation of Teaching Credit

Benchmark RVUs/year	Teaching adjustments
patient contact × 20% expected drop in productivity	When supervising
hours/year =	a medical student

Teaching adjustment × reported hours supervising medical students = RVU teaching credit

Example: For a faculty member who supervises medical students 200 hours/year:
3,100 RVUs/year
1,411 hours/year × 0.20 = 0.4349 RVUs/hour

0.4394 RVUs/hour x 200 hours supervising/year = 88 RVU teaching credits/year

Pay-Out Distribution

Base salary, academic supplement and administrative differential are paid out on a monthly basis. The clinical incentive is paid quarterly based on any work RVUs generated above those required to cover one fourth of the base salary. The teaching credit is paid at the end of the year. A sample annual salary calculation for two faculty with different responsibilities and productivity is shown in Table 4.

PROGRAM IMPLEMENTATION

After designing the basic components of the program, we devoted much effort to anticipating the effects of the program on various situations. For example, we looked at the possible effects on part-time faculty, salary-linked benefits and compensation during sick leave. We then described the program for faculty in a written document addressing each of these situations. We offered a transition period of either two or six months to each faculty member before starting on the program. Those already meeting productivity expectations—21 out of 35—were changed over after only two months, and all others after six months. During the transition period we provided education sessions on productivity terms, gave billing and coding workshops and described expectations and methods to enhance productivity.

Salary increases or decreases may occur on an annual basis if the $/RVU changes according to MGMA benchmarks. Faculty receive regular productivity reports, including feedback on individual and group performance. Faculty who are not generating enough work RVUs to cover their base salary are placed on probation for six to 12 months, after which the university makes a decision about continuing their appointments.

Table 4 Sample Salary Calculation for Two Physicians

Minimum RVUs required to cover base=2,170 RVUs/FTE/year (70% of benchmark)
Dollas per RVU conversion factor=$42/RVU

Salary Component	Physician A		Physician B	
	RVUs	Compensation	RVUs	Compensation
*Base	2,170	$91,140	1,736	$82,026
Academic supplement				$9,140
Administrative differential				$5,000
**Clinical incentive	980	$41,160	914	$38,388
Teaching credit				
(see Fig. 1)	88	$3,696	44	$1,848
Total salary		$135,996		$136,376

*RVU requirement adjusted based on percentage efforts.
**RVU generated in excess of minimum required to cover base.

Physician A is a full-time clinician who generates 3150 work RVUs/year. He spends 200 hours/year teaching medical students.

Physician B spends 80% of her time in clinical care and generates 2,650 work RVUs/year. She has a 10% administrative appointment for which she receives a $5,000 administrative differential and a 10% reduction in the minimum RVUs required to cover her base. Her remaining effort is covered on a grant-funded research project that supports 10% of her base salary. This amount is transferred to an academic supplement, and the RVUs required to cover this portion are dropped. She spends 100 hours/year teaching medical students.

Both leadership and faculty regard our compensation program as a success in our health system. In just nine months we have shown a 22 percent increase in productivity, twice that of other primary care divisions in this health system. At the same time, our salary costs increased only 3 percent, a rate equal to other divisions. The difference between the increase in productivity and the increase in salary cost occurred because several of our faculty had a guaranteed salary based on rank prior to the implementation of our program. These individuals had to increase their productivity substantially to earn the salary to which they had become accustomed.

After the program was established, only two faculty members left our division; both gave spousal relocation as a reason. The number and quality of educational sessions with students and residents remained unchanged.

DISCUSSION

We attribute the success of our program to several key elements:

- We were able to align the University of Michigan Health System goals of increased productivity, improved patient access and preservation of our teaching mission with our compensation plan;

- We defined key principles of valuing faculty effort in clinical care, education and research and used them to guide the design of the plan;

- The plan is based on sound data using national norms for both productivity and compensation;

- Each faculty member received a detailed implementation document that addressed the general plan and special circumstances;

- A transition period instituted before the plan's implementation allowed us to provide education sessions on productivity terms, expectations and methods to enhance productivity; and

- We had a dedicated administrative support team, regular feedback to faculty and a willingness to modify our plan with market changes.

Our plan does not yet address two important areas: direct linkage to cash flow and quality-of-care measures. Our plan emphasizes, and has been successful in, increasing productivity as measured by work RVUs. We have not yet investigated how this correlates with changes in net collections or cash flow. We might assume that increases in RVUs reflect increases in gross charges and patient volumes. If, however, the increase in RVUs comes at the expense of increased operational costs, the health system may not realize a net financial benefit. Further, in highly capitated markets, increases in visit numbers or RVUs may actually conflict with the financial goal of keeping the cost of care below the fixed monthly payment.

As we said, several measures for quantity of care delivered are readily available, but quality-of care-measures, especially for the pediatric population, are less abundant and less tested. Placing total emphasis on quantity of care runs the risk of negatively affecting quality. We intend to establish or identify key performance measures that allow us to link quality of care to compensation.

End Notes

1. Tenenbaum, D. Concocting a palatable compensation formula. Family practice management, 1994 October; 48.

2. Levitt, L; Holve, E; Wang, J; et al. Employer health benefits, 2001 annual survey. Menlo Park (CA): Henry J. Kaiser Family Foundation and Health Research and Educational Trust; 2001. Exhibit 2.6, 31. See www.kff.org.

3. The competitive edge 12.1—HMO industry report. St. Paul (MN): InterStudy Publications; 2001. www.interstudypublications.com.

4. Havlicek, PL. Medical groups in the U.S. Chicago (IL): American Medical Association; 1996. Table 8.4, 45.

5. Burke, MR; Kalogredis, VJ. Working capitation into your compensation formula. Family practice management 1996 March; 47.

6. Cejka, Susan. "Physician Compensation" audio conference. Medical Group Management Association, September 17, 1998.

7. Johnson, B. Polarity management: Identifying and managing unsolvable problems. Amherst (MA): HRD Press; 1996. 267 p.

8. Compensation models should be fair, understandable to be effective. Medical Group Management Update 1996 November 35 (11):8.

9. Levitt, L; Holve, E; Wang, J; et al. Employer health benefits, 2001 annual survey, Menlo Park (CA): Henry J. Kaiser Family Foundation and Health Research and Educational Trust; 2001. Exhibit 6.1, 75. See www.kff.org.

10. For a more complete discussion on quality measurements, see Issues in the management of physician services, from Integrating the practice of medicine. AHPi; 1997.

11. MGMA physician compensation and production survey. Englewood (CO): Medical Group Management Association; 2001.

12. Drucker, PF: The new productivity challenge. Harvard Business Review 1991 Nov/Dec; 69(6):6979-6985.

13. Levering, R; Moskowitz, M. The 100 best companies to work for in America. New York: Doubleday; 1993. 505 p.

14. McAdams, JL; Hawk, EJ. Organizational performance & rewards: 663 experiences in making the link. New York: American Compensation Association and Martiz Inc.; 1994.152 p.

15. Schuster, M. Forty years of scanlon plan research: A review of the descriptive and empirical literature. International Yearbook of Organizational Democracy, 1, 1983; 53-71.

16. Rosow, JM: Castner-Lotto, J; Hickey, JV. Participation, achievement, reward—Creating the infrastructure for managing continuous improvement: New York: Work in America Institute, Inc.; 1998. p.ix.

17. Information exchange questionnaire: Employee incentive plans. Medical Group Management Association 1999 February.

18. Dong-One, K. Factors influencing organizational performance in gainsharing programs. University of Wisconsin-Madison; unpublished paper; 1994

19. McAdams, J. Research from the trenches . . . Making group incentives work. Consortium for Alternative Reward Strategies IV; 1998.

20. Kohn, A. Punished by rewards: The trouble with gold stars, incentive plans, A's, praise, and other bribes New York: Houghton Mifflin Company; 1993. p. 190.

21. Eigen, L; Siegel, JP. The manager's book of quotations. New York: AMACOM; 1989. p.271.

22. Rosow, JM; Castner-Lotto, J; Hickey, JV. Participation, achievement, reward— Creating the infrastructure for managing continuous improvement. New York: Work in America Institute, Inc.; 1998. p.xi.

23. Gordon, T. Leader effectiveness training. New York: The Berkley Publishing Group; 2001. p. 6.

24. Taylor, FW. The principle of scientific management; 1911.

25. Rosen, RH. Leading people: Transforming business from the inside out. New York: Penguin Group; 1996.

26. Rosow, JM; Castner-Lotto, J; Hickey, JV. Participation, achievement, reward— Creating the infrastructure for managing continuous improvement. New York: Work in America Institute, Inc.; 1998. p. 55.

27. Ibid.

28. Fein, M. Improshare: An alternative to traditional managing. American Institute of Industrial Engineers; 1981. p. 27.

29. Ibid, p. 23.

30. McAdams, JL. The reward plan advantage. San Francisco: Jossey-Bass; 1996.

31. Davenport, R. The greatest opportunity on Earth. Fortune 1949 Oct.

32. Davenport, R. Enterprise for everyman. Fortune 1950; XLI (1), 51-58.

33. Scanlon, J, personal correspondence, Penn State University, Steelworkers Archives

34. Rosow, JM; Castner-Lotto, J; Hickey, JV. Participation, achievement, reward— Creating the infrastructure for managing continuous improvement. New York: Work in America Institute, Inc.; 1998. p. x.

35. Kim. Factors influencing organizational performance in gainsharing programs.

36. Rosow, JM; Castner-Lotto, J; Hickey, JV. Participation, achievement, reward— Creating the infrastructure for managing continuous improvement. New York: Work in America Institute, Inc.; 1998. p. 54.

37. Frost, C. Leadership in the new American workplace. Unpublished workbook.

38. McAdams, JL; Hawk, EJ. Organizational performance & rewards: 663 experiences in making the link. New York: American Compensation Association; 1994 Oct.

39. Scanlon, JN. Profit sharing under collective bargaining: Three case studies. Industrial and Labor Relations Review, 1948;2;58-75.

40. Kruse, D. Profit sharing: Does it make a difference? Kalamazoo: W.E. Upjohn Institute for Employment Research; 1993. p.vi.

41. Rosow, JM; Castner-Lotto, J; Hickey, JV. Participation, achievement, reward— Creating the infrastructure for managing continuous improvement. New York: Work in America Institute, Inc.; 1998. p. 54.

42. Ibid., p. xi.

43. Scott, KD; Floyd, J; Benson, PG; Bishop, JW. The impact of the scanlon plan on retail store performance; 2002. Unpublished research paper.

44. Bledsoe, DR; Leisy, WB; Rodeghero, JA. Tying physician incentive pay to performance. Health Care Financial Management, 1995;49(12):40-44.

45. Ibid.

46. Compensation monitor: Study shatters big myth about primary care compensation, Managed Care 1999:8,17.

47. Bell, H. The power of the bonus. Physician's Practice Digest 1999 Jan/Feb:18-20.

48. McMenamin, P; Heald, R, editors. Medicare RBRVS: The physician's guide. New York: American Medical Association; 1998.

49. Physician compensation and production survey report: 1998 report based on 1997 data. Englewood CO: Medical Group Management Association; 1998.

50. Shea, S; Nickerson, KG; Tenenbaum, J; Morris, TQ; Rabinowitz, D; O'Donnell, K; Perez, E; Weisfeldt, ML. Compensation to a department of medicine and its faculty members for the teaching of medical students and house staff. New England Journal of Medicine. 1996;334(3);162-7.

51. Sargent, J; Osborn, L. Resident training in community pediatrician offices: not a financial drain. American Journal of Diseases of Children 1990;144:1356-1359.

52. Curriculum for the M.D. degree: Overview, issues, recommendations. Ann Arbor (MI): University of Michigan Medical School Task Force; 1999.

Index

A

academic settings, 72, 133–139
access, 103, 110
administration
    differential component for, 137
    infrastructure of, 58–59
    time management of, 127
American College of Medical Practice Executives
    (ACMPE), 113
American Compensation Association (ACA), 77,
    93
American Medical Association, 3, 5–6, 8
ancillary services, 70. *see also* Stark laws
Arling, Bryan, 6

B

base-plus-incentive plans, 51–52
Baumgardner, Dwane, 84, 92
behavioral incentives, 101, 124, 126–127
benchmarking compensation, 11
benefits, 11
Beth Israel Hospital, 77, 81, 93
Blue Cross and Blue Shield, 1, 3
bonuses, 27, 78–79. *see also* incentive
    compensation
    distribution methods for, 36–38
    formulas for, 128–129
brainstorming, 66–67
Bryan, James E., 4
business literacy, 86–88

C

call schedule, 76
capitation, 9–10. *see also* managed care
    fee for service and, 38–43
    fixed/variable overhead model for, 74–75
Case, John, 86
Cejka, Susan, 9
Cejka and Associates, 9
citizenship, 57
clinical productivity, 54–56. *see also* productivity
coding, 30
collections, 31, 119–120
    compensation tied to, 126
    history of, 1–3
commitment, in gainsharing, 88–89
    competency and, 95–96

equity and, 91–95
participation and, 89–91
communication, 106
compensation principles, 7–9, 12–14. *see also*
    design process; legal issues
    alignment of incentives, 9–10
    correlation, 11–12
    information gathering for, 10–12
    plan examples, 15–18
competition
    within marketplace, 66
    within practices, 13, 105–106
    within specialities, 30
Consortium for Reward Strategies (CARS), 78–79
consultants, selection of, 127–128
Cunningham, Robert, III, 1, 4
Cunningham, Robert M., Jr., 1
current procedural terminology (CPT) coding,
    30

D

Davenport, Russell, 87
decision makers, 64, 102. *see also* design process
deferred compensation, 11
Deming, W. Edwards, 82, 84
design process, 12, 50–51, 64–68, 129. *see also*
    compensation principles
    for academic settings, 72, 134–139
    decision makers for, 64, 102
    example for hospital-owned groups,
        116–117
    external factors and, 32
    for hospital-owned groups, 71–72
    identifying need for, 63, 99–101, 123–124
    lowering compensation, 133–134
    for multispecialty groups, 70–71
    need for simplicity in, 13, 104, 130
    for nonphysician providers, 73–74
    for officers in medical practices, 75–76
    opting out of call and, 76
    for part-time physicians, 74–75
    for rural practices, 73
    for single speciality groups, 69–70
    "trial-and-error" approach to, 125
distribution formulas, 7, 31–32
doctor-patient relationship, 4–5
Donnelly Corporation, 77, 83–84, 93

145